RAISED IN
SPLENDOR

RAISED IN SPLENDOR

THE HOPE OF GLORIFICATION
FOR A SECULAR AGE

JASON B. ALLIGOOD

B&H
PUBLISHING®
BRENTWOOD, TENNESSEE

Published by B&H Publishing Group
Brentwood, Tennessee

Dewey Decimal Classification: 236.22
Subject Heading: FUTURE LIFE / HEAVEN / IMMORTALITY

Cover design by Faceout Studio, Jeff Miller.
Cover images by gg_tsukahara, camilkuo, Ezepov Dmitry /
Shutterstock. Author photo by Karis Doud.

1 2 3 4 5 6 • 28 27 26 25

To Amber, Jonah, Madelein, Karis, Trevor, Aubrey, and Tucker—I love you all more than you'll ever know

ACKNOWLEDGMENTS

I would like to thank my precious wife, Amber, who has not only encouraged me tremendously in the process of writing this book but has also endured a cancer diagnosis in the midst of it. You are my greatest earthly joy! My children and their spouses have been a monumental blessing as well. Jonah and Madelein, Karis and Trevor, and Aubrey and Tucker, thank you for always lifting my heart to King Jesus as we talk about life and your growth in Christ and desire to see your friends come to faith and walk closely with our Lord.

I would also like to thank the flock of Fellowship Bible Church. You have been a constant benediction to me in the midst of uncertain times and cheered me on as I wrote this work. I am grateful I do not serve the church alone and I am indebted to Steve Stocksiek, Mike Ducharme, Justin McMenamy, and Jonathan Peppers for their service to our people.

I would not have gotten very far in this project without the help of those from B&H who believed in it. Madison

Trammel is always a calming influence on my life, and I wish we had more time to hang out. Logan Pyron has served faithfully as my acquisitions editor and has become a dear friend. Eddie LaRow is not only a faithful member of FBC, but also a beloved friend and constant encouragement in my life. Thanks to these and all the others at B&H that made this publication possible.

Last, I want to thank our triune God whose beauty I long to see in the face of our Lord and Savior Jesus Christ, who bought me back from the slave market of sin with His own blood and will one day raise me to glory with Him by the same resurrection power that raised Him from the dead.

CONTENTS

FOREWORD

There is no mystery so dark as bearing the name of Christ. To follow Christ is to walk down a path with suffering waiting for you at every turn. And though some suffering will be inflicted by others, most suffering is self-inflicted. To be a Christian is to wake up each day and decide to crucify yourself all over again—I said this mystery is dark. For until you suffer the death of the self you cannot imagine what promise lays buried in Jesus's words when He says, pick up your cross, come, and die with me. Christianity must be the most morbid religion.

But Christianity is stranger still. For within this daily crucifixion is the hope of glory. We put our sinful passions to death with unrelenting fervor because our Lord was crucified, rose on the third day, and ascended into heaven. As Paul says, "Just as we have borne the image of the man of dust, we shall also bear the image of the man of heaven" (1 Cor. 15:49 ESV). Therefore, only by dying to ourselves do we live to Christ. John Owen was right: in mortification we find vivification.

We sometimes forget this is why Christ came in the first place, to clothe us with His image. In Adam, our nature was polluted. Reformed theologians do not exaggerate when they say depravity is so pervasive that our nature has been corrupted in Adam. But God, out of the abundance of His mercy, sent His only begotten Son to assume our nature so that in His glorification He might bring many sons to glory. Or, as Athanasius says in *On the Incarnation*, God became man "to bring the corruptible to incorruptibility."

But how long, O Lord? Our pilgrimage to incorruptibility has already begun. For the Holy Spirit has caused us to be born again, a regeneration that inaugurates the moral renewal of our nature in sanctification. And though the pilgrimage is a weary one, fraught with failure, it is not without progress. For that same Spirit is conforming us into the image of our crucified and risen Lord. Surely even Moses would have been jealous to discover that "we all, with unveiled face, beholding the glory of the Lord, are being transformed into the same image from one degree of glory to another. For this comes from the Lord who is the Spirit" (2 Cor. 3:18 ESV). With each crucifixion of the self is a resurrection that takes us higher up and higher in until glorification makes us shimmer with the holiness of Christ.

Each year legions of books on theology release, but how rare it is to see even one of them contemplate our future glory. Perhaps we have grown too comfortable in this world, forgetting the apostle Peter who said we are wayfarers. Did not Jesus say His kingdom is not of this world? He did. So why so few books longing for the inheritance of our heavenly kingdom? This book by Jason Alligood should be read for that reason alone, simply because we want nothing so much as to see God. For the apostle John tells us that when we see Christ we will—at last—be like Him (1 John 3:2).

But who can put words to this blessed hope? I would not trust anyone with this task. We need a theologian who knows suffering, and longs more than most for its relief in Christ. That theologian is Jason Alligood, reminding us that we will be "partakers of the divine nature, having escaped from the corruption that is in the world because of sinful desire" (2 Pet. 1:4 ESV). I've always thought the best theologians are the ones who can take the deepest mysteries and explain them with such clarity that the mystery becomes deeper still. That is where Jason Alligood leaves you in the end: fortified in the guarantee of the beatific vision, only to swim in the vast ocean of glorification's incomprehensibility.

There is no mystery so dark as bearing the name of Christ. But to be sure, there is no mystery so bright as a

Christian brimming from the light of Christ. For He is the radiance of the glory of God. In His light we see light.

Matthew Barrett

Professor of Christian Theology, Midwestern Baptist Theological Seminary

Editor-in-Chief, *Credo Magazine*

INTRODUCTION

This book is about hope. It's about the hope that Christians have for the future to one day dwell in the presence of the triune God (Father, Son, and Spirit) forever. It is about the hope of attaining the blessed vision of God's glory in the face of Jesus Christ. When we discuss this hope, we must be careful about how we do so on two fronts.

First, we need to take care that we have the right lens. What do I mean? One of the tragedies of our modern era is that books about hope tend to have the wrong object at their center. These kinds of books usually promote a man-centered view of theology rather than a God-centered view. The Bible gives us the proper God-centered lens when it says things like this: "The pride of mankind will be humbled, and human loftiness will be brought low; the LORD alone will be exalted on that day" (Isa. 2:11). Isaiah the prophet is speaking of the future day of the Lord and how the tendency of mankind to lift himself up above God will be brought to its proper place and God will be shown as the only One worthy of praise. Books about hope that put man in the center tend to talk about how God is concerned *most* about mankind's well-being. While I am not saying that God is unconcerned about mankind's well-being at all, I am saying that God is concerned *most* about His own glory. Again, Isaiah records the words of God saying, "I will act for my own sake, indeed, my own, for how can I be defiled? I will not give my *glory* to another" (Isa. 48:11, emphasis added). Notice that God says what He does is for His own sake and that He will not give His glory to anyone else. Therefore, when we think about the hope that God gives us, we must be clear that though we benefit from this hope—and benefit greatly from it—God does what He does for us for the sake of His name and glory.

The second matter is that we understand the biblical definition of hope. When we use the word *hope*, we typically mean that we have a strong desire to see something happen. For instance, we hope that our favorite baseball team wins the game against our storied rival. I am a St. Louis Cardinals fan, so when it comes to my hopes, I want to see my Cardinals defeat the Chicago Cubs. However, this is not the biblical definition of hope. The Bible speaks of hope as that which believers in Jesus Christ can be certain will happen because God has promised it. The author of Hebrews tells us that because of the sacrifice of Jesus and our trust in Him, we can draw near to Him. He then encourages the readers (including us!) to "hold on to the confession of our hope without wavering, since he who promised is faithful" (Heb. 10:23). Notice how the author tells us to both not waver in the confession of our hope and that we can hold fast to that hope because God is faithful to keep His promises. This biblical idea of hope centered around God's glory and His promises is what we want to work through together in this book.

The specific hope—the promise—on which we will focus is the hope of *glorification*. Perhaps you have heard this word in a sermon or read in a book somewhere that the Christian's salvation is composed of three factors: justification, sanctification, and glorification. One way or another you have likely heard these defined as justification (the sinner declared right standing before God because of Christ's perfect life, death and resurrection); sanctification (the believer progressively being made more holy, more like Jesus); and glorification (the believer coming into the fullness of their salvation, being made perfectly into the image of Christ, having their bodies redeemed and not having to deal with sin or its consequences any longer). The first two elements of this trifold paradigm of salvation have received a lot of attention over the last few decades. Sadly, the last one, glorification, has received less attention, thus the reason for the book that you hold in your hands today.[1]

---

1. I want to note here two works in recent days that are in line with our current study and that provide a great deal of help on the subject. The first is

As a Christian, I want you to not only understand and love the doctrines of justification and sanctification, but also that of glorification—how these doctrines are related, and what benefit glorification is in your life today as you await its fulfillment. I want you to not only understand that you will see the beauty of our triune God in the face of Jesus at His appearing, but also to know how this hope shapes your Christian life every day until that glorious day arrives. I want you to know and worship our triune God more as we study through the lens of His glory being ultimate even as we speak of the glory that we will share with Him one day. Having these things in mind, allow me to show you how we will proceed through this book.

The first chapter will deal with the definition of glorification and why it matters in the life of a Christian. In other words, my desire is to explain why having the hope of

---

Graham Cole, *Glorification: An Introduction* (Wheaton: Crossway, 2022). Dr. Cole released this book as I was working on attaining a contract for the current work. As my book intends, Dr. Cole's work is for an audience that is lay level to pastoral with a good theological understanding. I commend it to you. The second work, which is far more academic, is Haley Goranson Jacob, *Conformed to the Image of His Son: Reconsidering Paul's Theology of Glory in Romans* (Downers Grove, IL: InterVarsity, 2018). Though her work certainly contains theology, it falls more in the category of Biblical Studies. It is excellent, as well. Besides these two works, there are works in the Biblical Theological realm that address issues related to Creation, Fall, Redemption, and Consummation, but a full systematic treatment has not been published since Bernard Ramm, *Them He Glorified* (Grand Rapids: Eerdmans, 1963), which is now out of print.

glorification is essential for your faith today. Chapter 2 will explore creation and the way in which God created us in His image for His glory and what that creation meant for the glory of mankind before we fell into sin. Chapter 3 will deal with mankind's fall into sin and how we view ourselves considering God's glorious standard. Chapter 4 will show how salvation is much more than just receiving forgiveness of sins (though it is not less!), but it is also a promise to receive all that is ours in Christ, including our union with Him. We will highlight the benefits of union with Christ, including His glorification. Chapter 5 will position us to see that God Himself is the treasure of eternity, providing an explanation of how our glorification readies us to dwell in His triune presence forever. Considering the two previous chapters, chapter 6 will show how the hope of glorification compels the believer to live a holy life now in anticipation of what is to come. And last, chapter 7 will explain how our hope for what is to come in glorification motivates hope in the daily turmoil of our lives as those who walk by faith and not by sight.

I want to emphasize again what follows brings light to the eyes of the believer about their future hope—all of this is through the lens of the worship and glory due to the Father, Son, and Spirit who is blessed forever! Amen.

GLORIFICATION: WHAT IS IT AND WHY DOES IT MATTER?

"Our Lord Jesus Christ . . . through His transcendent love, [became] what we are, that He might bring us to be even what He is Himself."[1]
—Irenaeus of Lyons

I like to read the writings of old dead guys. The quote that begins this chapter is from one of my favorites among them. His name is Irenaeus, and it is said that he was a

---

1. Irenaeus of Lyons, "Irenaeus against Heresies," in *The Apostolic Fathers with Justin Martyr and Irenaeus*, ed. Alexander Roberts, James Donaldson, and A. Cleveland Coxe, vol. 1, The Ante-Nicene Fathers (Buffalo, NY: Christian Literature Company, 1885), 526.

student of Polycarp who was a student of the apostle John.[2] My fascination with Irenaeus is his proximity to John who walked with Jesus in His earthly ministry and therefore through Irenaeus's writings we get close to the theology of the early church outside of the Scriptures. His way of writing is not as familiar to those of us who live 2,000 years removed from him, but nonetheless there is great benefit in reading what he has written, especially in light of Scripture.

Considering Irenaeus's quote above as we think on the scriptural and theological idea of glorification, we get a glimpse of the early church's view of the doctrine. Let me expand on this quote a bit. Jesus Christ, the eternal Son of God, put on humanity, lived a perfect life, died in the place of sinners, and rose again so we can be reconciled to a holy and triune God and so He can bring us into that eternal resurrection life just as He has resurrection life. There are quite a few theological ideas to unpack in this sentence, and it is important that we do so to get a solid definition of glorification. Let me begin by zooming out a bit and using familiar terminology.

As I mentioned in the introduction, the doctrines of justification and sanctification have gotten much attention

2. For a quick overview of Irenaeus and his life, see *Irenaeus: A Guide to His Life and Writings*, ed. Jessica Parks, Faithlife Author Guides (Bellingham, WA: Faithlife, 2017).

in recent years. I have no contention with this emphasis as these doctrines are ones that are easily misconstrued and threaten the very heart of the gospel. We should hold to the biblical idea of justification and sanctification as from God's grace alone, through Christ alone, by faith alone. Yet, we must also rejoice in what God says about those whom He has justified. As Paul says, in Romans 8:30, "Those [God] justified, he also glorified." The past tense of "glorified" here instills us with the hope for what *will* happen. There is a promise here from God through the writing of Paul that those whom God has justified—those who God through Christ has declared right standing with Him—will certainly be glorified. The word for *glorify* here means "to cause to have splendid greatness" or "clothe in splendor."[3] Even with these definitions, we don't truly get a clear idea of what glorification is, and we need to understand such a promise of glory in the context of the rest of what Paul tells us here.

---

3. S.v., δοξάζω, (2) BDAG, 3rd ed. Haley Goranson Jacob suggests that being conformed to the image of the Son must be more than mere "splendor/ radiance or the visible manifest presence of God," but rather that has to do with being "conformed to his status and function as the Son of God who rules over creation." While I do not want to take on her entire argument, I do think we cannot say that being conformed to the image of God is any less than having some idea of splendor or radiance and also being in the presence of God's glory, or better the experience of the beatific vision, but it could be more, as Jacob suggests. See Jacob, *Conformed to the Image of His Son: Reconsidering Paul's Theology of Glory in Romans* (Downers Grove, IL: InterVarsity, 2018), 10, 224–25.

Earlier in the same passage Paul states that God has "predestined [believers] to be conformed to the image of his Son" (Rom. 8:29). This conformity to the image of His Son is the sense in which we must take this idea of being clothed in splendor. The ways in which believers will be conformed to the Son's image needs further consideration, and we will certainly explore this idea more in chapters 4 and 5. But for now, let's look at one more verse that is pertinent to our understanding of the hope of glorification at this point. Paul, in speaking of our heavenly citizenship, says, "[Christ] will transform the body of our humble condition into the likeness of his glorious body" (Phil. 3:21). Paul tells us that our glorification is not merely a characteristic conforming, but rather the entirety of who we are, body and soul will be changed. Here we come to an idea of what has been called the "already/not yet." The idea of already/not yet is a way to state that there are aspects of our redemption that are already complete, but also aspects of our redemption that are not yet, that which we await. In this case, we say our spirits/souls have been regenerated and our new man is being renewed day after day (already), but glorification also entails the transformation of our lowly bodies into ones fashioned for glory (not yet). Thus, we see an example of what this glorification entails, something we must come back to time and again in our study.

John Gill, a great post-Reformation pastor and theologian, helps our understanding when he speaks of this conforming of the believer into the image of Christ not as conformed to His image as the eternal Son of God, but rather:

> conformity to Christ in his *human nature*, both here and hereafter: here in holiness; the image of God was in man, in his first creation, this is defaced by sin; and in regeneration, the image of Christ is instamped, his grace is wrought in them, his spirit is put into them, to enable them to walk in him, and after him: this will be *complete hereafter*, and will consist in perfect holiness, being freed from the very being, as well as the power and guilt of sin; in perfect knowledge of every thing that will tend to their happiness; and in glory like to Christ, both in soul and body.[4]

Notice how Gill speaks with that "already/not yet" language I mentioned earlier. Here it is concerning the reality

---

4. John Gill, *An Exposition of the New Testament*, vol. 2, The Baptist Commentary Series (London: Mathews and Leigh, 1809), 494. Emphasis mine.

of union with Christ as the basis not only of justification and sanctification, but glorification as well. We will explore this idea of union with Christ more in chapter 4, but for now, I want us to see the "golden chain of salvation" as some have called it: that those who God justifies, and sanctifies, He will also glorify.

A Definition of Glorification

All of what we have seen thus far leads us to the need of a succinct definition of glorification that we can refer to throughout our study. *Glorification is the final stage of the triune God's overarching work of salvation in believers in which He fully conforms them to the image of the glorified human nature of the Son and by which they will be totally free from sin and its effects.*

Let's break this definition down to grasp exactly what we're talking about here.

Salvation's Final Stage

When I say above, "Glorification is the final stage of the triune God's overarching work of salvation," we are reminded of those three phases of salvation: justification, sanctification, and glorification. These three are inseparable but should not be mixed or confused. First, God justifies us, declaring us as righteous because of the work of Christ. God credits the righteousness of Christ to us and we are therefore declared right standing before God. He also sanctifies the believer, making the believer more like Jesus, more holy. He is beginning the work of making us into the image of Christ now. Justification, however, is not sanctification. Those who are justified will be sanctified.

As I mentioned above, we see in Romans 8 that those who God justifies, He also has predestined for them to be conformed to His Son's image. In our life as Christians, we become more like Jesus as God works in our hearts and we submit ourselves to His Spirit. As an old Baptist confession says, "Those who have been regenerated are also sanctified by God's word and Spirit dwelling in them. This sanctification is progressive through the supply of Divine strength, which all saints seek to obtain, pressing after a heavenly life in heartfelt obedience to all Christ's commands."[5] The reason these cannot be mixed is because of the absolute nature of justification versus the progressive nature of sanctification. We must not think of justification as progressive, because God has already declared us as just because of Christ's finished work. As the Reformed theologian

---

5. Abstract of Principles, XII. "Sanctification," see https://www.sbts.edu/about/abstract/.

Louis Berkhof states, "Justification is a judicial act of God, in which He declares, on the basis of the righteousness of Jesus Christ, that all the claims of the law are satisfied with respect to the sinner."[6]

Additionally, we must not think of our justification as dependent on our sanctification. It works the other way around; we are continually being made more like Jesus because it is His righteousness that makes us holy. John Owen once said, "our Sanctification is an effect or fruit of what [Jesus] did and suffered for us."[7] In the same way, we cannot think of our glorification as dependent on our sanctification, because it is our right standing with God because of Christ that ensures that we will be glorified (Rom. 8:28–30).

However, this final stage is yet to occur; we are not yet glorified. We are awaiting God's promise to glorify us. We have confidence that He will do this because He has already justified us and is currently conforming us into the image of His Son and the work of this conforming will not be complete until He returns for us. Turning to Berkhof again, "When we speak of sanctification as being imperfect in this life, we do not mean to say that it is imperfect in parts, as if only a part of the holy man that originates in regeneration

---

6. Louis Berkhof, *Systematic Theology* (Grand Rapids: Eerdmans, 1938), 513.

7. John Owen, *The Doctrine of Justification by Faith through the Imputation of the Righteousness of Christ* (London: R. Boulter, 1677), 221.

were affected. It is the whole, but yet undeveloped new man, that must grow into full stature."[8] This truth then leads us to a key verse for our understanding. The apostle John tells us that, "We know that when he [Christ] appears, we will be like him because we will see him as he is" (1 John 3:2). Since this final stage is the heart of our book, we will come back and investigate this truth more. But for right now, I want us to understand what the "final stage of salvation" means.

Conformed to the Glorified Human Nature of the Son

Along with this idea of the final stage of salvation, we add that we will be conformed to the glorified human nature of the Son. If we think about 1 John 3:2 as stated above, we see the overlap of the final stage and the idea of what our glorification will be like. John tells us earlier in this same verse that "what we will be has not yet been revealed." But we do know that when we see Him as He is we will be like Him. Gill asserts above that this will be in accordance with Christ's humanity. We think again of Paul's statement in Philippians 3:21, that our bodies in their current humble condition He will transform "into the likeness of his glorious body."

---

8. Berkhof, *Systematic Theology*, 537.

However, a glorified body is not all there is to glorification, but it is the aspect of salvation that signifies the final full conforming to the image of the Son.

The Scriptures also declare that we currently "have the mind of Christ" (1 Cor. 2:16). We must see this aspect of our current condition as true, but not fully formed, in the sense that because we have not yet reached glorification, our minds are still weighed down with our unredeemed flesh. Progress as we might in our sanctification and growing as we might in our holiness and Christlikeness, we still await the finality of glorification. What has changed now is that we see the world through the "lens of Christ," if you will.[9]

The Lord Jesus Christ: Two Natures, One Person

Here we must take a bit of an aside to explain something about the dual natures of the incarnate Christ. In the incarnation, the eternal son of God assumes a human nature to become like us, to live a perfect life as a human and die the death that we deserve, and He was raised again to show His victory over sin and death and to be the firstfruits of a

---

9. See Wendell Will, "The 'Mind of Christ' in 1 Corinthians 2:16," *Biblica* 70, no. 1 (1989): 110–22.

human resurrection that will set the pattern for the rest of the redeemed (1 Cor. 15:1–23).

Therefore, the incarnated Son of God has two natures, one human and one divine, but He is only one person; He is truly God and truly man. The eternal Son of God has always existed as just that, the eternal Son. Theologians talk about the Son being eternally begotten from the Father meaning the Father communicates the divine essence to His Son from eternity. We must be careful here in understanding this "begottenness" of the Son as an *eternal* reality. By virtue of this truth, the Son is and has always been of the same essence as the Father. The Father, the Son (and the Spirit) share the exact same nature. However, in the Son coming to the earth in the incarnation, He assumes a second nature, a truly human nature. This happens via the miraculous work of the triune God in the virgin birth through Mary. Jesus assumes a human nature and takes on all the qualities of true humanity without sin (Heb. 4:15).

We distinguish between Christ's human nature and divine nature here to keep the proper Creator/creature distinction in us even though we argue for Christ's incarnation as truly God and truly man. In other words, I would argue that we participate in the divine nature of God by way of the Spirit conforming us to the image of Christ who is the image of God (2 Cor. 4:4). This perhaps invokes thoughts of Adam being made in the image of God. Adam was related to God from God's making Adam (Creator) in His image (creature). This not only sets Adam apart from the rest of creation, but also puts him in special relation to the Creator.[10] This image was not destroyed when mankind fell, but certainly it was corrupted by sin—not meaning that the image itself was corrupted, but rather that Adam was then a fallen man who imperfectly images God and therefore needed restoration in some sense.[11] Therefore, it is through our participation in and conforming to Christ who is the God-Man that we become partakers in the divine life.

Now having a proper understanding of the dual natures of Christ's personhood after the incarnation, we must investigate the way in which He lived to show what we mean when we say that we will share in the glorified human nature of Jesus. To explain this truth, we must look at four aspects of Jesus's incarnated life: His active and passive obedience, His victory over sin and death, and His glorified nature.

---

10. This idea begins to work itself out in the way we also understand Adam's relation to the rest of humanity, specifically federal headship, which we will address in chapters 2 and 3.

11. John Kilner argues that people are damaged because of the fall, but not the image of God. See *Dignity and Destiny: Humanity in the Image of God* (Grand Rapids: Eerdmans, 2015).

His Active Obedience

Can you imagine what it must have been like for Mary and Joseph to watch Jesus grow? Luke records that Jesus grew in stature and favor with God and men (Luke 2:52). Likewise, the author of Hebrews tells us that Jesus lived life like we do, yet without sin (Heb. 4:15). Theologians call this His active obedience. Active obedience describes Jesus fulfilling the law where Adam failed. He lived His life perfectly as a Jew (which Israel had failed to do). He did this without ever sinning, even though He experienced external temptations to sin (Heb. 4:15; Matt. 4). This obedience is true even to the point of death upon the cross (Phil. 2:8). Louis Berkhof helpfully states:

> God continued to demand obedience of man, but in addition to that required of him that he pay the penalty for past transgression. Meeting this double requirement was the only way of life after sin entered the world. If Christ had merely obeyed the law and had not also paid the penalty, He would not have won a title to eternal life for sinners; and if He had merely paid the penalty, without meeting the original demands of the law, He would have left man in the position of Adam

before the fall, still confronted with the task of obtaining eternal life in the way of obedience. By His active obedience, however, He carried His people beyond that point and gave them a claim to everlasting life.[12]

His active obedience is an expression of His righteousness which is imputed (credited) to us when we trust in Him. When God looks at believers, He sees Christ's righteousness and—as I state above—God declares us righteous. This righteousness is ours in this present life (2 Cor. 5:21; 1 Cor. 1:30), but though we are declared righteous in this life, we do not experience the fullness of righteousness without sin until our glorification. However, because we are united to Christ in this way, it guarantees that our glorification will be similar to His human glorification because Christ has secured this reality for us in His active obedience.

His Passive Obedience

In His life and death, Jesus perfectly obeyed God's Law and in obedience to the triune will. What He did passively is receive the reality of humanity in His body, which is especially seen in His trials and crucifixion. We should understand

---

12. Berkhof, *Systematic Theology*, 381.

passive obedience as those things Jesus received in His human nature from others. As Louis Berkhof states, "His passive obedience consisted in His paying the penalty of sin by His sufferings and death, and thus discharging the debt of all His people."[13] Further Berkhof says that Christ's sufferings:

did not come upon Him accidentally, nor as the result of purely natural circumstances. They were judicially laid upon Him as our representative, and were therefore really penal sufferings. The redemptive value of these sufferings results from the following facts: They were borne by a divine person who, only in virtue of His deity, could bear the penalty through to the end and thus obtain freedom from it. In view of the infinite value of the person who undertook to pay the price and to bear the curse, they satisfied the justice of God essentially and intensively. They were strictly moral sufferings, because Christ took them upon Himself voluntarily, and was perfectly innocent and holy in bearing them.[14]

---

13. Berkhof, *Systematic Theology*, 381.
14. Berkhof, *Systematic Theology*, 381.

Though Christ actively submitted Himself to the triune will in His humanity, there were things done to Him by others which He received in His mortal body. Peter displays this best when he says to the crowd at Pentecost, "Though he [Jesus] was delivered up according to God's determined plan and foreknowledge, you used lawless people to nail him to a cross and kill him" (Acts 2:23).

This Victory Over Sin and Death

When we take Christ's active and passive obedience together, we come to the crux of the matter concerning what Christ had to do in order to redeem people from every tribe, tongue, and nation. Further, the reason that Christ took on humanity is that only He was able to reconcile mankind to the triune God. His perfections as truly God are expressed in His sinlessness as a true man and in His undeserved death for the sake of those who did. And by taking on the sin of those for whom He died, He is able to be the offering for sinners that God accepts (2 Cor. 5:21). He becomes the righteousness for sinners, as God looks upon Christ's perfect life and sacrifice and declares them righteous because of Him. Not only is this defeat of sin true at the cross, but its defeat along with death's is also true at Jesus's resurrection (1 Cor. 15).

When the Bible tells us that Jesus rose from the dead, this is not like any resurrection we have seen previously. When Jesus raised Lazarus from the dead, Lazarus would one day die again. Lazarus's resurrection was not permanent. However, when Jesus is raised by the trinitarian will, it is a firstfruits kind of resurrection. Jesus is the first of any human to be raised in final resurrection. We get a glimpse of what it means for us to receive a resurrection that fits us for eternity with God.

Paul tells us in 1 Corinthians 15 that we will share in the resurrection body like Christ. Paul explains that "Flesh and blood cannot inherit the kingdom of God, nor can corruption inherit incorruption" (15:50). We should immediately recognize the problem with this. We are flesh and blood. We have corruptible bodies. As someone who is coming up on fifty, I feel this more and more. I used to be a skateboarder. I was no Tony Hawk, but still an honest to goodness ollie-popping skater. It was only a few years ago that I could still take a fall or even ride a board for that matter without feeling the aches and pains of age. However, not a day passes where my knees don't ache when I get out of bed, likely due to those years of skateboarding. The point is, we know that our flesh is corruptible, every time we bump our shin into a coffee table or sit in the hospital room with a friend who is dying of cancer. We can't get way from the reality of our mortality; it confronts us every day.

What then are we to make of Paul's statement that these flesh-and-blood, corruptible bodies cannot inherit the kingdom of God? Thankfully Paul front-loads and back-loads this question in the very text from where we draw our question. Earlier in the passage Paul tells us that just as we are heirs of Adam according to his fleshly body—"The first man was from the earth, a man of dust," those who are in Christ are like the "second man [who] is from heaven" (1 Cor. 15:47–48). In other words, we receive our corruptible human bodies from Adam, and we will receive our imperishable glorified bodies from God through Christ's resurrection. The truth concerning the resurrection body of Jesus leads us to thinking about Christ's glorified nature.

His Glorified Nature

One of the reasons it is so difficult for us to conceive of glorification is that Scripture does not give us a wealth of information on our glorified state. However, we can look to Jesus's glorified state and seek to glean as much as we can from Him.

Here we return to the resurrection of Jesus to begin understanding glorification. Paul states our relation to

Christ—our union with Him—in His resurrection body in terms of image-bearing (1 Cor. 15:47-49). He uses the two scriptural representatives of mankind as the grounding of our understanding. Paul states that we who are made in the image of Adam are made of dust, and that Jesus's origins are from heaven, therefore He is the man of heaven whose image we will bear as resurrected believers. Paul submits that, "Flesh and blood cannot inherit the kingdom of God, nor can corruption inherit incorruption" (v. 50). Paul did not say that flesh and blood *will not* inherit the kingdom of God, but rather that our flesh and blood as it exists today *cannot* inherit the kingdom of God. There must be a transformation—our corruptible and mortal bodies must be clothed with incorruptible and immortal qualities (vv. 53-54).

Paul's basis for saying this is that Christ's resurrection body has taken on these qualities (15:49). Just as in our old creation bodies in Adam we were created in dust, so in our new creation resurrected bodies we will bear the image of the Man of Heaven.

Free from Sin and Its Effects

Even though Christ never sinned, we still do. We are sinners. Indeed, this is why Christ had to come to redeem us from our sin, and yet we still deal with the effects of sin, though we are free from sin's slavery (Rom. 6:18). Even as Paul talks about the justification, sanctification, and glorification of believers in Romans 6, he then is very transparent about the struggle of sin that is real for the believer in Romans 7. In short, Paul states that there are times when he is so frustrated because he does the things he doesn't want to do, while also not doing the things he desires to do.

If we are believers in Christ, we get this struggle! Yet, at the end of this Paul says something very important. He asks a rhetorical question that gives a framework for the hope of which we are speaking in this book. After all of this talk of desiring to do what God commands and yet still recognizing this principle of flesh that is waging war against the principle of God's law, which he as a Christian now desires to do in his heart he says, "Who will rescue me from this body of death?" (Rom. 7:24). Paul's response is one of thanksgiving, hope, and joy: "Thanks be to God through Jesus Christ our Lord!" (v. 25). Paul is saying (as he writes this letter to the Romans under the inspiration of the Spirit) that there is coming a day when believers will no longer deal with sin, nor a body that is weighed down by sin.

Sin affects both the wear and tear of our bodies as well as the ability for us to resist it. Usually when I hear folks talk about their glorified bodies, they typically are referring to the first of these ailments. This is our own sort of passive affliction, though we can do damage to ourselves for sure. Most believers recognize that at our glorification we will no longer have to deal with the aches and pains brought about because of sin, but how often are we thinking about the active sin in our hearts and minds that will be eliminated at our glorification? This is what drives Paul's exuberance. In one place he minimizes the aches and pains that are far outweighed by the glory that is to come {2 Cor. 4:17), but here he emphasizes the full and final freedom from sin that we will experience, because we will share in the glorified life of Christ as we have outlined above.

Essential to Our Faith

We have considered what glorification is and sought to show throughout why this hope is important for the life of the believer. As we close this first chapter, I want us to bring together some of these elements and express why the hope of glorification is essential to our faith.

The author of Hebrews says that "faith is the reality of what is hoped for, the proof of what is not seen" (Heb. 11:1). As I state above, when we rightly observe hope as the Bible explains it, we are not talking about wishful thinking, but rather a confidence in what will occur. The hope of glorification is essential to our faith because faith believes the promises of God. This side of the cross and resurrection of Jesus we fit into the category of those who believe having not seen the risen Savior. This idea comes from the infamous scene where the apostle Thomas says he will not believe Christ has resurrected until he sees and touches the nail prints in Christ's hands or put his hand in the side where Jesus was pierced. Jesus appears to all the apostles, and Thomas exclaims, "My Lord and my God!" In blessing Thomas, Jesus says, "Because you have seen me, you have believed. Blessed are those who have not seen and yet believe" (John 20:25–29). We fit in the latter group. Though we have not seen, we nevertheless believe. The object of our faith is a person, the Lord Jesus Christ, and He promises He will come again for us and receive us unto Himself and we will be with Him always (John 14:3). And further, and really crucial to our study in this book, when we see Him, we will be like Him (1 John 3:2). This is the reality of what we hope for and the proof of what is not yet seen. And yet, it is important to note that even our glorification in and of itself is not the end to which we hope. It certainly is a very important piece, but ultimately this transformation readies us for the greatest part of our hope: the experience of the beatific vision, that is the blessed revelation of our triune God in His glory.

A Brief Explanation of the Beatific Vision

Though we will address this idea further in chapter 6, we cannot move on without a bit of explanation here. You may be unfamiliar with the terminology "beatific vision," or might have only heard of it in some sort of high church context. If you do not know this expression, I want to explain it here, and if your experience is the latter, I would like to gently correct you of the notion that the doctrine is relegated to non-Protestant religion.

There are disagreements over what exactly the beatific vision entails. Will we see the essence of God? Or will we see the glory of God in the face of Jesus Christ? These options are but two amongst a few. Again, we will explore this concept more fully a bit later in our study, but what is important now is to establish a definition as the goal of the believer's glorification.

In short, the vision of God is the believer being able to behold God in His glory without the hinderance or consequences or effects of sin. It will be the fullness of experiencing 2 Corinthians 3:18 and Revelation 21:23 which read respectively, "We all, with unveiled faces, are looking as in a mirror at the glory of the Lord and are being transformed into the same image from glory to glory; this is from the Lord who is the Spirit," and "The city does not need the sun or the moon to shine on it, because the glory of God illuminates it, and its lamp is the Lamb." What we begin to experience here in our justification and sanctification is culminated in our glorification when we dwell in the heavenly city on earth that is consumed with the light of the glory of God and in which we will see Him in all His glory.

Beyond this aspect, we will also see Jesus as He is in all His glory, and in His face see the glory of the triune God. Seeing Jesus in His glorified state is the embodied vision of God.[15] As I show earlier, 1 John 3 gives us this hope when the Evangelist states, "We know that when he appears, we will be like him because we will see him as he is." In the context of John's letter, as well as the rest of the New Testament, it is unmistakably Jesus who appears. It is in Jesus's appearance that we will surely begin to see the fullness of God's glory even as we will continue to as we walk with Him. Revelation 21:3 states, "God himself will be with them and will be their God." Certainly, we will experience the presence of God in the glory of His essence (whatever that may be), but we are also promised the embodied presence of the Son. It is He who will return bodily for us (1 Thess. 4:13–18) and we will dwell with Him in the same way. This idea goes back to our

---

15. Hans Boersma states, "On my understanding, to see Christ is to see the essence of God." Hans Boersma, *Seeing God: The Beatific Vision in Christian Tradition* (Grand Rapids: Eerdmans, 2018), 51.

earlier statement that the eternal Son who is truly God put on flesh and became true humanity and dwells in a glorified humanity forever.

Conclusion

For one to claim to be a believer and who does not have a hope for glorification and all that it entails is to miss out on an essential part of our faith. If we focus only upon the benefits of our salvation for the here and now, we miss the fullness of what God will do and the longing we should have in anticipation for being in God's presence and beholding His glory and being free from sin and its consequences. I believe that much of this has to do with the prosperity of living in the West, where we are, for the most part, well off compared to the rest of our brothers and sisters around the world. We measure out our comfort in material possessions and numb ourselves with entertainment. The point is that we rarely think about glory and our glorification or even more so beholding God's glory because we seem to not have a need to long for them. Some have coined this lack of longing as an over-realized eschatology, meaning that even if one does not say it out loud, they are fine with not thinking about a future glory because everything is well and fine here and now. Someone who thinks along these lines is not thinking of the trajectory on which justification sets the believer. Again, reminding ourselves of Paul's statement, "those whom [God] justified, he also glorified" (Rom. 8:30).

It is perhaps because those of us in the West do not normally suffer as Christians have in the past or presently do elsewhere in the world that we do not focus much upon the hope of glorification in our everyday lives. There is an old saying with which you are likely familiar: he is so heavenly minded that he is no earthly good. The implication of this statement is that the believer who focuses on the hope of glorification is daydreaming about the glorified state and therefore has nothing to offer in the current earthly state. This idea seems to betray the materialistic attitude I mentioned above. As Michael Allen states in the introduction to his book, *Grounded in Heaven*, "Not surprisingly, Christians in various situations of oppression and struggle have cherished the heavenly minded intonations of the biblical testimony."[16] He goes on to submit that this kind of hope stokes the faithfulness of living for Christ in the present day.[17] We might adjust the old saying to something new: that person is so heavenly minded that they do the *most* earthly good. The hope of glorification should not be some

---

16. Michael Allen, *Grounded in Heaven: Recentering Christian Hope and Life on God* (Grand Rapids: Eerdmans, 2018), 15.
17. Allen, *Grounded in Heaven*, 15–17.

"out there" concept that is not seen as an essential part of the faith of believers. There is an incredible hope of glorification that shapes our lives here and now.

For us to examine this concept well, we now need to turn to the creation of mankind in God's image as the beginning of humanity's existence and the grounding of our glorified reality.

CREATED FOR GLORY

*"When human souls have become as perfect
in voluntary obedience as the inanimate
creation is in its lifeless obedience, then they
will put on its glory, or rather that greater glory
of which Nature is only the first sketch."*[1]
—Clive Staples Lewis

The quote above by the famed atheist turned Christian author, better known by his abbreviated name C. S. Lewis, invites us to consider the topic of our second chapter. The imagery of this statement by Lewis stokes a backward look to humanity's original created glory with the hint of a forward look to the glory that is to come.[2] Perhaps like me,

---

1. C. S. Lewis, *The Weight of Glory* (1949; repr., New York: HarperCollins, 2009), 43.
2. Lewis is not saying that the obedience of the saints is how they receive glorification, but rather that due to what God has done for them in

you grew up in Sunday school. I am showing my age a bit here, but the church I grew up in used flannelgraphs to help illustrate biblical stories for us. Essentially, there were little characters cut out of flannel and hung on a flannel background. When thinking about the story of creation, as the teacher would use these illustrations, I would try to imagine beyond the little characters what it must have been like for Adam and Eve to live in perfect relationship with God. This side of mankind's fall into sin was hard for me to grasp, and as I have grown older, I have come to realize there was much more to what God expresses through Moses than what I was often taught. Even as adults, we tend to rush through Genesis 1–3 and miss some of the nuance of what is there. So, I think it's important for us to unpack more of the meaning both in this chapter and the next to help us see exactly what God intends in these first few chapters. We should begin by looking at the triune God as the Glorious Creator and His glorious creation.

The Glorious Creator and His Creation

For us to rightly examine humanity's glorious creation by God (and the rest of creation to which Lewis points us),

---

justification and sanctification results in an ultimate perfect obedience at glorification.

we must go back to the beginning, really before the beginning, to the only One who exists eternally before creation and time. Indeed, the Bible takes us here when we open to its first page. You are familiar with it no doubt, "In the beginning, God . . ." (Gen. 1:1). Before anything was, God *is*. We must get this concept of *what* God is before we can proceed with what God created.

The Westminster Larger Catechism asks, "What is God?" and gives the response:

> God is a Spirit, in and of himself infinite in being, glory, blessedness, and perfection; all-sufficient, eternal, unchangeable, incomprehensible, every where present, almighty, knowing all things, most wise, most holy, most just, most merciful and gracious, long-suffering, and abundant in goodness and truth.[3]

This question may seem strange, "*What* is God?" but it precisely raises an important category distinction that we discussed earlier, the Creator/creature paradigm. When we think of what God is, we must think of Him as totally other than us. As we will see, we are made in God's image, not

---

3. Westminster Larger Catechism, Question 7, https://www.freepresbyterian.org/uploads/Larger_Catechism.pdf.

Him in ours. God's eternal existence as the triune One who is in and of Himself self-existent reminds us that He is not dependent on anyone or anything. As Stephen Charnock submits, "[God] was before all things, and, therefore, depends upon no other thing."[4] This truth highlights the distinction between the Creator and the created. We as the creature are totally dependent on God. God is self-sufficient. As this self-sufficient one, God also in His infinite wisdom creates. And when God creates, He declares all things good (Gen. 1). God attributes goodness to His creation because He Himself is the very essence of good. And in the same way that God creates everything good, it is also therefore glorious as it reflects His own glory. Bavinck expresses this truth stating, "Scripture . . . says that all of nature is a revelation of God's attributes and a proclaimer of his praise."[5]

That God is our creator reminds us that He is worthy of our worship. Charnock once again helpfully says, "The first ground of worship we render to God is the infinite excellency of his nature, which is not only one attribute, but results from all; for God as God is the object of worship."[6] And though God is worthy of worship, the point I am

---

4. Stephen Charnock, *The Existence and Attributes of God* (Grand Rapids: Baker, 1979), 1:321.
5. Herman Bavinck et al., *Reformed Dogmatics: God and Creation*, vol. 2 (Grand Rapids: Baker Academic, 2004), 2:433.
6. Bavinck, *Reformed Dogmatic*, 1:284.

presenting is that God does not need our worship as if He was lacking anything, even before He created. Therefore, as we gaze back at creation, God is before it and is completely satisfied in His triune nature as Father, Son, and Spirit; "In the beginning, God." We see this idea exemplified by Paul with his doxological reflection in Romans 11:33–36 where he states:

> Oh, the depth of the riches and the wisdom and the knowledge of God! How unsearchable his judgments and untraceable his ways! For who has known the mind of the Lord? Or who has been his counselor? And who has ever given to God, that he should be repaid? For from him and through him and to him are all things. To him be the glory forever. Amen.

Our attention is drawn to the middle section in which Paul asks rhetorical questions related to the nature of God: Who has known the mind of the Lord? Who has been God's counselor? Who seeks repayment from God after giving to Him? The implied answer to these questions is "no one!" In other words, no one can sit down with God and say, "Look, God, You've got it all wrong. I know the way You think and work and this just doesn't work out so well, all this grace and wrath, and justice and mercy aren't going to fly." No one can rightfully call into question God's ways. It is not that people will not call these ways into question, but they cannot rightfully do so. This truth has to do with the Creator/creature distinction we discussed above. Once again, we are made in God's image, not Him in ours. Everything in God's creation is His to do with as He pleases (according to His holy will) and, He has given mankind stewardship over the earth and possessions, but even when we give back to God, we are giving back what is already His. We cannot say to God, "You owe me!" Therefore, what we give—even worship—is not repayment.

Paul responds to this truth by reinforcing the triune God's self-sufficiency stating, "For from him and through him and to him are all things." Notice the word "for." Paul explains the inability of man to question God as creator. The summary of this statement is what theologians call the simplicity of God: God is, and God is Father, Son, and Spirit, equal in essence and yet eternally distinguished as Father, Son, and Spirit. The concept of divine simplicity may be foreign to you and so, to give a brief definition: divine simplicity is the theological idea that the triune God is not composed of parts. As Ronni Kurtz submits, "there is nothing in God that is not God."[7]

---

7. Ronni Kurtz, *No Shadow of Turning: Divine Immutability and the Economy of Redemption* (Fearn, Ross-shire, UK: Christian Focus Publications, 2022), 152.

We then see the phrase "from him." Nothing exists without God. Nothing existed before God, and nothing existed until God called it into existence. As above, we are committed to understanding that God has no beginning and no end and thus He is uncreated; He is Creator. Therefore, as Paul states here everything is from Him. This truth is what we call creation *ex nihilo* (out of nothing). As Moses writes, God is there in the beginning before anything is created. God spoke and the nonexistent began to exist. "God said, 'Let there be light,' and there was light (Gen. 1:3). The original language conveys the idea of something like this: God spoke light and there was light. Once again turning to the early church, Irenaeus states, "it is necessary that things that have come into being have received the origin of their being from some great cause; and the origin of all is God, for He Himself was not made by anyone, but everything was made by Him."[8]

Then we take notice of Paul's phrase, "through him." Nothing has come to pass except that which God has decreed from eternity past, and ordained for His purposes, to bring glory to Himself and good to His own people. Nothing falls outside of God's decree and God decrees all things by His eternal Son. So, we begin to see that we should have a trinitarian understanding here in this verse. It is

---

8. Irenaeus, *On the Apostolic Preaching* (Crestwood, NY: St. Vladimir's Seminary Press, 1997), 42.

through the Son that He "[sustains] all things by his power-ful word" (Heb. 1:3).

Paul then finally says, "to him." Everything is ultimately for God's glory. He knows the end from the beginning and is glorified in it. This concept is impossible to grasp. Considering this notion is like standing at the edge of the Grand Canyon and looking toward the bottom and knowing that there's a bottom and being able to get glimpses of the bottom, but the details are beyond our understanding. In a much grander way, God is and all that exists is "to Him!" All that exists is for His glory and we conclude that the Holy Spirit as being eternally from the Father and the Son exalts the Godhead in the application of God's sovereign will in the world.

We must then understand this truth of God as Creator as one which implies consummation as well. That which God created He will bring to its rightful and glorified end— even when mankind has sinned and brought destruction and decay to it (as we will explore closer in our next chapter). Geerhardus Vos (a great Reformed Dutch theologian of the nineteenth and twentieth century) puts it this way, God "cannot abandon the works of his hands . . . he must perfect what he has begun."[9] Putting a finer point on how God as

9. Geerhardus Vos, *The Eschatology of the Old Testament* (Philipsburg, NJ: P&R Publishing, 2001), 7.

Creator relates to our current study, He is also the consummator of creation which He will bring to its glorified reality. As we consider the way in which the Bible begins, we must also consider how it ends. The apostle John highlights this parallel when he relays his vision:

> Then I saw a new heaven and a new earth; for the first heaven and the first earth had passed away, and the sea was no more. I also saw the holy city, the new Jerusalem, coming down out of heaven from God, prepared like a bride adorned for her husband. Then I heard a loud voice from the throne: Look, God's dwelling is with humanity, and he will live with them. They will be his peoples, and God himself will be with them and will be their God. (Rev. 21:1–3)

We will explore these truths in chapter 5, but for now, I want to show how God as Creator relates to God as Consummator and the bringer of glory to His creation.

Having established God as a glorious creator (and consummator), we must see that all which He creates reflects His glory. Therefore, concerning mankind's creation, David says that in creating man, God "crowned him with glory and honor" (Ps. 8:5). Mankind's stature according to this psalm is below God and the angels, but that God places mankind above and over creation (Ps. 8:6). Indeed, the Scriptures declare that "God created man in his own image; he created him in the image of God; he created them male and female" (Gen. 1:27).

Created in God's Image

The doctrine of mankind being created in God's image (*imago Dei*) continues to help structure our study of God's glorious creation. This special creative element sets mankind apart from the rest of creation. Rather than speaking mankind into existence, as God does with the rest of creation, God forms mankind from the dust of the ground (already created matter) and breathes life into him (Gen. 2:7). Thomas Boston calls God's creation of mankind "the masterpiece of lower creation."[10] By "lower," Boston means to communicate earthly instead of heavenly, mankind over against the angels. If mankind is the masterpiece of God's earthly creations, we must also investigate what this means. Mankind is set apart from the rest of God's creative work on earth in that He is the only one created in the image of God

---

10. Thomas Boston, *The Whole Works of the Late Reverend and Learned Mr. Thomas Boston* (Aberdeen, Scotland: George and Robert King, 1848), 1:177.

(*imago Dei*). The image of God in mankind has been a matter of much debate over the centuries. So, what is the *imago Dei*?

One way that believers work through theological questions is to think about what something is not, to help us think about the truth of that thing.[11] We may ask what is not true about the image of God in man? First, we should state, it is not true that the *imago* is God creating little gods. That is, there is only One God who is triune in nature, and completely other than His creation (Gen. 1; Deut. 6:4). We are not so invested with God's image that we are gods in some deified sense.[12] Second, the image of God is not something that is tied to the intellect of humanity alone. In other words, if mental capacity is a benchmark for the image of God in mankind, then we must say that those with diminished mental states are somehow lesser bearers of it. The same could be said of other so-called communicable attributes of God, such as creativity or the like, meaning that those with diminished capacities in any of these qualities would lack proper bearing of the image. These examples are just

---

11. In philosophy this is called negation, particularly in stating what something is not to emphasize what is true.

12. There are times when the Scriptures are translated in such a way that they speak of mankind as "gods" (e.g., John 10:34–39), however, it is not in the sense of true deity. See John Calvin and William Pringle, *Commentary on the Gospel according to John* (Bellingham, WA: Logos Bible Software, 2010): John 10:34.

a couple of ways that mankind has sought to describe the *imago Dei* that fall short of keeping it intact in all of humanity—which I believe is necessary to keep mankind as the special and crowning of God's creation.

While we cannot invest the time and space to work through the various views of what constitutes the image of God, I think that John Hammett and Katie McCoy capture a good and biblical summary stating that the image of God "involves the gift of a capacity for a particular type of personal relationship; primarily with God."[13] Since there is much debate over the exact meaning of the *imago Dei*, let us then settle where the confessions have settled and let other works sort out the finer meanings that do not suit our purposes here. The Second London Confession states: "After God had made all other creatures, He created man, male and female, with reasonable and immortal souls, rendering them fit unto that life to God for which they were created; being made after the image of God, in knowledge, righteousness, and true holiness."[14] We should examine a couple of these phrases more closely.

---

13. John S. Hammett and Katie J. McCoy, *Humanity*, Theology for the People (Nashville: B&H Academic, 2023), 116. I would recommend this recent book as a helpful work on the topic of theological anthropology.
14. Second London Confession of Faith (hereafter known as 2LCF), 4.2, http://baptiststudiesonline.com/wp-content/uploads/2008/08/the-second-london-confession.pdf.

Reasonable and Immortal Souls

With the expression "reasonable and immortal souls," we see one aspect of being made in the image of God. All the rest of God's creation does not possess the qualities of reasonable and immortal souls (at least not in the same degree as humanity). The combination of reasonable and immortal says something about which the authors of the confession understood concerning the makeup of mankind. As James Renihan explains concerning this phrase, "The whole purpose of man's creation is that he would be capable of a life lived with, before and to God."[15] Though all of creation certainly declares the glory of God (Ps. 19:1-7), only mankind relates to God specifically in the way of a reasonable and immortal soul. When God created mankind in His image and likeness, He created them as creatures of reason. Far above the rest of creation, God instills in mankind a knowledge of nature and Himself. For example, after God creates Adam, He gives him dominion over the earth and charges him with the naming of the animals (Gen. 2:19). The animals do not name themselves, but God instructs Adam to do so with the reason and authority God gives him. As Adam is naming the animals, he reasons that

---

15. James Renihan, *To the Judicious and Impartial Reader: Baptist Symbolics,* vol. 2 (Cape Coral, FL: Founders Press, 2023), 137.

though there are male and female companions amongst the animals, there is not one found who befits him (Gen. 2:20). Furthermore, it seems that reason given to mankind by God is expressed in the law written on their hearts by which God also commands them to obey (Rom. 2:15; Gen. 2:15–17).

Also concerning mankind being made after God's likeness, just as His Spirit is eternal, mankind's soul is everlasting. Scripture teaches us that when mankind dies, though his body returns to dust, his spirit (or soul) is with the Lord (Gen. 3:19; 2 Cor. 5:8). When the believer is resurrected, their transformed and glorified body will reunite with their soul. Their dead body needed resurrection, but their soul lived on, because it is immortal (1 Thess. 4:13–18). Paul speaks of the decay of the outer man (which needs resurrection) but of the renewal of the inner man, the soul, which lives on.[16] We will explore later what Renihan means by a *life lived with, before and to God.* But for now, let us consider the next phrase.

---

16. Portions of this section were used in my article "What Is the Soul?" for the series Theology in the Everyday, https://ftc.co/resource-library/articles/the-soul/, September 6, 2023.

Knowledge, Righteousness, and True Holiness

We must then understand the makeup of mankind's soul as we consider the phrase, "being made after the image of God, in knowledge, righteousness, and true holiness." These three elements must be seen as reflective of God and not eternal as God is in and of Himself. In other words, mankind can only reflect these as a creature since he is not the Creator. Of these three descriptions Boston says concerning knowledge, "He was created wise: Not that he knew all things . . . [but] he had all the knowledge that was necessary for life and godliness," concerning righteousness, "There was perfect conformity in his will to the will of God," and holiness, "Man's affections were pure and holy . . . loving what God loved and hating what He hated; loving and delighting in God with all his heart, strength soul and mind."[17]

We must tread carefully here regarding what happens to the image of God after the fall, something we will consider in greater detail in the next chapter. But for now, we should express that the *imago Dei* is exclusively descriptive of mankind and that God intends for mankind as made in

---

17. Boston, *Works*, 1:182–83.

His image for the purpose of His glorious plan. We move on to this purpose now.

Created with a Glorious Purpose

As we have shown, the end of all creation is the glory of God and so each part of creation is meant to glorify God. Since mankind is the crown of God's creation, he too must have a glorious purpose; mankind's purpose must exceed the rest of creation. God gives this purpose in calling mankind to a two-fold vocation when He tells them, "Be fruitful, multiply, fill the earth, and subdue it" (Gen. 1:28). This call upon mankind once again demonstrates the unique place he has over creation (Gen. 1–2; Ps. 8:6–7). We then must answer not only what this vocation is, but also what it has to do with our glorification. Let us separate and examine this two-fold vocation.

Be Fruitful, Multiply, and Fill the Earth

When God tells mankind to be fruitful, multiply, and fill the earth, He is speaking of procreation. As with all the rest of God's creation, there is a reproductive quality in God's growing creation. Just as the animals were to reproduce after their kind, humanity is to reproduce after its kind. This reproductive activity is both commended and commanded by God. Basil sees this as in concert with the rest of the command of dominion: that mankind was to proportion the multiplying and filling of the earth so that for one part it is "useful for habitation, another part is necessary for cultivation, and the rest for the grazing of [animals]."[18] He goes on to summarize saying, "This is the blessing, this is the legislation, this is the honor given us by God."[19]

From our perspective of fallenness it may be difficult for us to grasp such an honor, but such is the case before sin enters the world. As we shall see in a moment, the purpose in this aspect of the command is the broadening of the kingdom and worship of God, especially before the fall.

Subdue the Earth

With the command to subdue the earth, we once again see that God is giving mankind dominion over creation. Mankind is the chief creaturely head over creation to bring order to his domain under God's rule. Meredith Kline says, "By investing man with the divine image, God appointed

---

18. St. Basil the Great, *On the Human Condition* (Yonkers, NY: St. Vladimir's Seminary Press, 2005), 42.
19. St. Basil the Great, *On the Human Condition*, 42.

him to privileged status over the rest of creation."[20] There is debate concerning what this subduing involves. At the very least, mankind is not to allow the earth to rule over him. Mankind is to care for the garden and the extension of it to the ends of the earth to cultivate it for mankind's use as the dwelling place of God and man. Work therefore is not a result of mankind's fall, but rather a part of God's intention for mankind before sin even enters the world. Kline again is helpful stating, "The cultural mandate put all the capacity of human brain and brawn to work in a challenging and rewarding world to develop the original paradise home into a universal city."[21]

As a part of this task and tending to the dwelling of mankind and God (the garden of Eden), mankind clearly has the opportunity to obey God and thus escalate His glory to another level; namely to expand that dwelling to the ends of the earth. However, there is also the possibility of condemnation at the failure of man's obedience, as we shall see. Before we look at the outcome of either of these scenarios, we should first contend that the overarching goal in God's creation of mankind in His image and His appointment of

---

20. Meredith G. Kline, *Kingdom Prologue: Genesis Foundations for a Covenantal Worldview* (Eugene, OR: Wipf & Stock Publishers, 2006), 18.
21. Cultural mandate is shorthand for God's command that mankind should be fruitful, multiply, fill and subdue the earth. Kline, *Kingdom Prologue*, 70.

him as His earthly caretaker is ultimately the worship of
God Himself.

The Goal Is Worship

Why did God command mankind as just described? As
we saw earlier, God as Creator deserves worship, and all of
creation is directed as a worshipful homage to their Creator.
Humanity, as those created in God's image, has a greater
duty to direct this worship. Scholars have shown that the
directives that God gives to Adam and Eve essentially point
to the cultivation of worship to God. Adam is the one who
God appoints as the main worship facilitator in the garden.
G. K. Beale and Mitchell Kim summarize this idea stating,
"God placed Adam and Eve in Eden to work it and keep it
(Gen. 2:15), a priestly work in the Garden-temple of Eden.
His 'work' is not only working the soil (Gen. 2:5) but serving
God (e.g., Deut. 4:19), and he keeps the garden (Gen. 2:15)
as he keeps God's commands (see Lev. 18:5) and guards it
from pollution and corruption (see Num. 1:53)."[22]

---

22. G. K. Beale and Mitchell Kim, *God Dwells Among Us: A Biblical Theology
of the Temple* (Downers Grove, IL: InterVarsity, 2014), 24. The idea of
Garden-temple and Edenic-priest ideas are also found in such works as
Stephen G. Dempster, *Dominion and Dynasty: A Theology of the Hebrew
Bible* (Downers Grove, IL: InterVarsity, 2003), and T. Desmond Alexander,

Certainly, as we consider the image-bearing character-istic of mankind, the idea that worship as the priority of the garden is right. This worship is characterized by the holiness and purity of God and His deserving of such a place of honor in the garden and in the lives of His image-bearers. Adam's chore is keeping the garden as God had created it (Gen. 2:15). However, Adam's charge is not mere gardening, as J. V. Fesko says, "Read within the greater context of Scripture, Adam's responsibilities in the garden are primarily priestly rather than agricultural."[23] Alexander also implies this concept when he says, "Adam was commissioned to keep or guard the garden so that it would remain holy. This was a normal task associated with the sanctuary."[24] Further, there is a relational, yet worshipful aspect as Beale and Kim state: "Eden is pre-sented as a sanctuary and place where God dwells . . . Even the seemingly casual mention of God 'walking' in the gar-den of Eden (Gen. 3:8) is rich with connotations that suggest God's presence in the temple."[25] Considering these truths, we should not diminish the beauty and lush nature of Eden. Thomas Boston beautifully paints the dwelling of God and

---

From Eden to the New Jerusalem: An Introduction to Biblical Theology (Nottingham, England: InterVarsity, 2008).

23. J. V. Fesko, *Last Things First: Unlocking Genesis with the Christ of Eschatology* (Fearn, Ross-shire, UK: Christian Focus Publications, 2007), 71.

24. Alexander, *From Eden to the New Jerusalem*, 26.

25. Beale and Kim, *God Dwells Among Us*, 18.

man within the garden when he says, "Man had a life of pure delight and unalloyed pleasure. . . . Rivers of pure pleasure ran through it. The earth . . . was now in its glory; nothing had yet come in to mar the beauty of the creatures."[26]

Worship of God is the goal. Adam and Eve's obedience to God's mandate fulfills a worshipful end. As they go about the task of filling and subduing, they produce a worshipful environment. As God's representatives upon the earth, humanity produces more worshippers and spreads that worship throughout the world. Further, it seems best to understand that during their probation had they succeeded in their task they would have achieved an escalation of their existence with God as well. This is signified in the two trees which God presents to them in the garden, as we shall explore next.

Life and Death in the Garden

God presents two trees to Adam and Eve, one which brings death and one which brings life. Scripture identifies these as the tree of knowledge of good and evil and the tree of life. The authors of certain Protestant confessions have

---

26. Thomas Boston, *Human Nature in Its Fourfold State* (1720; repr., London: Banner of Truth, 1964), 51.

distilled these polar trees into statements like the one the Second London Confession states:

> God gave to Adam a law of universal obedience written in his heart, and a particular precept of not eating the fruit of the tree of knowledge of good and evil; by which he bound him and all his posterity to personal, entire, exact, and perpetual obedience; promised life upon the fulfilling, and threatened death upon the breach of it, and endued him with power and ability to keep it.[27]

Though the confession does not expressly name the tree of life, the implication of the promise of life is present in the idea of perpetuation in what God says concerning it in Genesis 3:22, "Since the man has become like one of us, knowing good and evil, he must not reach out, take from the tree of life, eat, and live forever." Because the keeping of God's law unto life was dependent upon Adam's obedience, it seems that the perpetuation of life was guaranteed in mankind eating from the tree of life. Vos states it thusly,

> Through the significance of the tree [of life] in general its specific use maybe distinguished.

---

27. 2LCF, 19.1.

It appears from Gen. 3.22, that man before his fall had not eaten of it, while yet nothing is recorded concerning a prohibition which seems to point to the understanding that the used tree was reserved for the future, quite in agreement with the eschatological significance attributed to it later. The tree was associated with the higher, the unchangeable, the eternal life to be secured by obedience throughout his probation.[28]

Although we know the outcome of these choices, we must reflect upon the reality of the choice and what that means for God's glorious purpose for mankind had Adam obeyed. Boston argues, "He promised him also eternal life in heaven, to have been entered into when he should have passed the time of his trial upon earth and the Lord should see [fit] to transport him into the upper paradise."[29]

What Thomas Boston and others have stated is that there was an opportunity for mankind to advance beyond the initial innocence of the garden into a glorified state. The status of mankind at creation was that he was without sin with the ability to sin. The truth of the glorified state is that

28. Vos, *Biblical Theology*, 28.
29. Boston, *Human Nature in Its Fourfold State*, 47.

mankind will be without sin and without the possibility of sinning. Boston believed the possibility of sinning speaks of mankind's original righteousness as mutable, and thus, he could have chosen sin, which he did. But had mankind stood firm throughout the probation, he would have been granted eternal life. If we look ahead to the perfect life of Christ, we understand that He won for us that which Adam lost and so we rest in His perfect righteousness and His resurrection life and glorified state becomes ours by His virtue. We look at these truths in coming chapters, but for now we are looking at how Adam could have secured this for humanity and thus escalate mutable righteousness to immutable had he passed his probation.[30]

Conclusion

From our studies thus far, we know that God had a glorious purpose in all of His creation and a great purpose of displaying His glory through His image-bearers. The point of this glorying of God through mankind was that mankind would mediate this glory through obedience to God's mandate, which was to have dominion over the creation through subduing it and multiplying himself throughout it.

---

30. Boston, *Human Nature in Its Fourfold State*, 43–45.

If mankind had obeyed, God would have eventually granted eternal life and mankind and his progeny and even the creation itself would have entered a glorified state in which mankind would dwell with God in full perfection.

We know, of course, that Adam failed to uphold this righteous state and instead gave into the serpent's temptation and fell from his innocent condition. Thus, humanity went from being without sin with the possibility of sinning to being sinful without the possibility of not sinning. It is this fall from glory that we look at next.

3

THE FALL FROM
GLORY

*"You ought to have turned away from the [serpent]
and said to him, 'Be off, you are a cheat, you
do not know the force of the direction given us,
nor the extent of the enjoyment we have, nor
the abundance of good things given us.'"*[1]
—John Chrysostom

John Chrysostom is another one of my favorite fig-
ures from church history. He, like me, was a pastor-
theologian. Much of Chrysostom's theology comes through
his sermons. The quote above provides a glimpse of his
theological musings as he preaches through Genesis 3.

---

1. S. John Chrysostom, *Homilies on Genesis 1–17*, edited by Thomas P.
Halton, translated by Robert C. Hill., vol. 74, The Fathers of the Church
(Washington, DC: The Catholic University of America Press,1986), 211–12.

We should take a closer look at what this passage and Chrysostom's quote has to do with glorification.

Tempted by a Lie

If it is not obvious, Chrysostom's comment is to Eve amid the serpent's attempt to deceive her. Genesis 3:1-3 reads, "Now the serpent was the most cunning of all the wild animals that the LORD God had made. He said to the woman, 'Did God really say, "You can't eat from any tree in the garden"?' The woman said to the serpent, 'We may eat the fruit from the trees in the garden. But about the fruit of the tree in the middle of the garden, God said, "You must not eat it or touch it, or you will die."'" In the quote above, Chrysostom is stating what Eve should have said in response to the serpent rather than what she did say.

The lie with which Satan tempts Eve is the question "Did God *really* say?" It is the word *really* that sows a seed of doubt. As Calvin says, "[Satan] wished to inject into the woman a *doubt* which might induce her to believe that not to be the word of God, for which a plausible *reason* did not manifestly appear."[2] Jesus states emphatically that Satan is the father of lies (John 8:44) and a crafty deceiver. And

---

2. John Calvin and John King, *Commentary on the First Book of Moses Called Genesis*, vol. 1 (Bellingham, WA: Logos Bible Software, 2010), 148.

with Eve, he seeks to sway the woman's belief that God has good intentions for mankind in what He has commanded. At minimum the lie is "there is a better and more satisfying way than God's way." This is seen more fully in the serpent's statement that God does not want to share His God-status with anyone, when he says, "God knows that when you eat it your eyes will be opened and you will be like God, knowing good and evil" (Gen. 3:5). The implication is that God is withholding something from Eve.

Here is the touchpoint with our study: God has declared everything He has created as good. When God creates mankind, He steps back as it were and says, "it is very good." Everything that God has done in creating is perfectly good and worthy of praise. God has even given man one who is like him for man not to be alone. As Chrysostom says, Adam and Eve should have recognized "the extent of the enjoyment," given to them, and "the abundance of good things." The deception to which Adam and Eve fall is that God has not given you *every* good and perfect gift; there is more, and you are missing out. The greatest part of the lie is that it misses out on the chief point, which is that God and the worship of Him as Creator is the center of what they experience in the garden. They are rightly related to God with nothing to hinder. Mankind "was made upright that is straight with the will and law of God, without any irregularity in his soul."[3] It seems that their normal way of life was "walking" with God (Gen. 3:8). We get a picture from this statement of "walking" and from what we saw in our last chapter that this relationship with God is a worshipful one. We think of the Creator and His creation, mankind being the pinnacle of His creation and then dwelling in harmony with God because sin has not entered the picture. As I said in chapter 2, there is good reason to believe that the garden of Eden prefigures the temple of Israel as the place where God's presence dwells and mankind worships.

Beyond the goodness of relating to God rightly, God also gave mankind every other tree in the garden to tend and enjoy. God's good gifts are those things that are within the bounds of His holy will (James 1:16–17). God had not left Adam and Eve with nothing. He had given them first the garden and then all the earth as their domain if they had obeyed and been fruitful and multiplied and filled it. God gave them each other. He would have given them children. God gave them the capacity to love Him and each other innocently. The animals were theirs to enjoy, the beauty of creation was theirs to cultivate and through which to reflect God's glory. Ultimately, God had given Adam and

---

3. Thomas Boston, *Human Nature in Its Fourfold State* (London: Banner of Truth, 1964), 38.

Eve Himself as the One to whom they should believe that He has every good for them and worship Him because of not merely the gifts, but more so Him as the Giver.

Instead, Adam and Eve rebelled against God, believing that God was holding something back from them. When we look further into the events, we realize what Adam and Eve had as their normal existence in the garden. Moses tells us that, "the man and his wife heard the sound of the LORD God walking in the garden at the time of the evening breeze, and they hid from the LORD God among the trees of the garden" (Gen. 3:8). It seems best to understand this walking with God as what the first couple experienced regularly in their daily lives. If not, they would be unfamiliar with this sound. Though we may not fully grasp this experience—who knows what exactly this walking with God was like. Suffice to say, it is an experience of God's presence unhindered by sin before mankind rebels. Once again Beale and Kim are helpful here when they say, "The imagery of Eden paints a compelling picture of the satisfaction of basic human desires in God's presence."[4] This satisfaction is what they gave up in the search of something better, which was not something better at all, but rather a deception.

---

4. G. K. Beale and Mitchell Kim, *God Dwells Among Us: A Biblical Theology of the Temple* (Downers Grove, IL: InterVarsity, 2014), 19.

The Glory That Could Have Been

It is an interesting exercise to imagine what could have been had Adam succeeded in the commission God gave Him. As is often true with the Devil's lies, they contain half-truths. Our first parents dwelling with God and worshipping Him in perfection would have brought advancement to their understanding of who they were and who God is. Adam and Eve's innocence and sinlessness did not mean that they were perfect in their understanding. For instance, before God created Eve, He instructed Adam to name the animals. Adam learns something from this. God declares that it is not good for man to be alone, but before He gives Adam a suitable helper, He has Adam name the animals and the Scripture tells us that as Adam is doing this, he realizes that there are pairs, male and female of these animals, and yet there is not one who fits with him. Adam learned something from the task that God had given to him.

We can therefore imagine a way in which God would have instructed Adam and Eve concerning their vocation that would lead to a greater glory than their original created state. Recall the words of the Second London Confession which states:

> God gave to Adam a law of universal obedi-
> ence written in his heart, and a particular

precept of not eating the fruit of the tree of knowledge of good and evil; by which he bound him and all his posterity to personal, entire, exact, and perpetual obedience; promised life upon the fulfilling, and threatened death upon the breach of it, and endued him with power and ability to keep it.[5]

It is the line "by which he bound him and all his posterity to personal, entire, exact, and perpetual obedience; promised life upon the fulfilling" that comes into focus for us here. The idea that the confession puts forth from the biblical data is that if Adam had obeyed, at some point God would have not only granted him the life he was currently living, but eventually eternal life. As Richard Barcellos observes, "Adam was not created in a condition or state that could be called 'glory' and he fell short of it by sinning. He failed to attain that state because he sinned. In other words, Adam was created in a state that could have been improved, with God being the ultimate cause and Adam's obedience the instrumental cause of that improvement."[6] In this same vein, Thomas Boston lists three types of life that are secured by Adam's obedience: natural life, spiritual life, and eternal

5. 2LCF, 9.1.
6. Richard Barcellos, *Getting the Garden Right: Adam's Work and God's Rest in Light of Christ* (Cape Coral, FL: Founders Press, 2017), 70.

life.[7] The first two speak of that which is true of Adam and Eve at creation. Their natural body and their spiritual union with God as those made in His image would have continued on as they were when God created them. The third, eternal life, speaks to an escalation of their entire person into the "celestial paradise," as Boston says.[8]

Another aspect of this escalation of humanity beyond created glory is tied to the concept of mankind's ability to sin. Mankind, in his original state of created innocence, has not sinned but still has the capacity and capability of sinning. When God gives His command to Adam, there is the expectation of obedience but with the possibility of Adam's disobedience as we see when God warns that Adam would die if he did eat from the tree of knowledge of good and evil. The difference for those who are glorified is the possibility of sinning will not exist. It seems best to understand had Adam and Eve obeyed God's mandate at the time God granted them eternal life that it would no longer be possible for them to sin. If we hold that this escalation was the potential for mankind from initial creation and before sin, we should maintain that the glories of the eternal state of which we await would have been theirs. Therefore, it seems

---

7. Thomas Boston, *The Whole Works of the Late Reverend and Learned Mr. Thomas Boston* (Aberdeen, Scotland: George and Robert King, 1848), 1:233.
8. Boston, *The Whole Works*, 1:233.

plausible to attribute the same to Adam and Eve had they succeeded that which Thomas Boston writes concerning the eternal state, "They will be so refined from all earthly dross, as never to savor more of anything but of heaven. Were it possible for them to be set again amidst the ensnaring objects of an evil world, they would walk among them without the least defilement."[9]

Beyond the escalation of humanity, we can also imagine that the Edenic paradise not only expands but becomes escalated as well. When God gives the commission to Adam and Eve to multiply and fill the earth, there seems to be an ideal way in which this would occur in the pre-fall world. Adam and Eve, in their innocence, would care for the garden, procreate, and those children would also cultivate and expand the boundaries of the garden. As Beale and Kim argue:

> Outside of the Garden-sanctuary of Eden lay a chaotic inhospitable area, God calls Adam and Eve not only to "work and keep" the Garden of Eden . . . but also to expand the Garden and "fill the earth." . . . God wanted to expand that sacred space and dwelling

---

9. Boston, *Human Nature in Its Fourfold State*, 438. Spelling has been updated.

place from the limited confines of . . . Eden to fill the entire earth. As Adam multiplied children in his image then they would expand God's dwelling place of his presence into the chaos outside of Eden until it filled the earth, and the whole earth reflected God's order and his glorious presence.[10]

But this does not seem to be the ultimate end of this effort. It is also possible to suppose that if Adam had succeeded at his calling to the degree that was satisfactory to the covenant, God would have escalated Adam's work into a glorified state. Here we merge the idea from the confession that God would have given Adam eternal life had he obeyed God's command with the idea that the expansion of the garden to the ends of the earth brings about the ultimate existence of God with man in a "unique city."[11] This unique city may have taken on all the characteristics of what Scripture eventually describes as the new heaven and new earth, but we do not know that for certain. What we do know is that God would have continued to dwell with mankind and for that dwelling to be eternal, there would need to be eternal characteristics to match. As Michael Allen argues, "the glitz

10. Beale and Kim, *God Dwells Among Us*, 34.
11. T. Desmond Alexander, *The City of God and the Goal of Creation* (Wheaton, IL: Crossway, 2018), 30.

and glimmer involve not only the natural order and architectural beauty of the New Jerusalem but also the relational harmony of a land without tears. And yet again, the central word is not one of newness but of nearness."[12] In other words, whatever the glorified earth may have looked like had Adam not sinned, the hope is not in the beauty of the dwelling place, but the beauty of the triune God dwelling with humanity. We are reminded again of the worshipful nature of our hope. The glory of new creation is not centered in the beauty of the trimmings of the place itself, but they rather reflect the beauty of the God who dwells there. Adam, however, did not keep the covenant God made with him, and therefore sin came into the world.

Sin Came into the World

The sad reality is that because of Adam's sin, rather than an escalation to glory, mankind was plunged into a world that is deeply affected by sin and therefore mankind is described both as sinner and sinful (Rom. 5:12). In the Old Testament the word for sin carries the idea of missing the mark, and in the New Testament the word signifies the transgression of a law. As we consider our study, a pertinent expression

---

12. Michael Allen, *Grounded in Heaven: Recentering Christian Hope and Life on God* (Grand Rapids: Eerdmans, 2018), 35.

of both ideas is found in Romans 3:23, "For all have sinned and fall short of the glory of God." "Fall short" means to fail to reach. Some have styled Romans 3:23 as failing to reach God's glorious standard. Of course, this is what Adam did at the fall, and as he federally represents humanity (a concept we will explore later), we too fall short, not only because we sin, but because we are sinners (Rom. 5:12).

As Paul writes, "sin entered the world through one man, and death through sin" (Rom. 5:12). Death is the great enemy of mankind that keeps them from knowing God rightly. Paul writes earlier in Romans that though God can be known through what God has created, mankind rejects this knowledge of God because of their sin (Rom. 1). Paul further states that "the wages of sin is death" (Rom. 6:23). Sin not only separates mankind from a right relationship and therefore a right knowledge of God, but that there is also a payment for that sin. A Holy God cannot ignore sin and refuse justice. As Berkhof states, "[God] maintains Himself as the Holy One and necessarily demands holiness and righteousness in all His rational creatures."[13] In the absence of such holiness and righteousness, there must be a punitive response. Therefore, Berkhof further states, "Punishment is the penalty that is naturally and necessarily

---

13. Louis Berkhof, *Systematic Theology* (Grand Rapids: Eerdmans, 1938), 256.

due from the sinner because of his sin; it is, in fact, a debt that is due to the essential justice of God."[14]

Sin, then, has consequences that are both temporal and eternal. We see the temporal consequence of sin almost every day. As I write this chapter, I am sitting in a cancer infusion center as my wife receives chemotherapy. Though her situation is not as bad as others, the reality of sin's destruction has hit close to home in the last few months. There is the reality of broken relationships and broken bones. There is the reality of that of which one is robbed or that which one steals. There is the consequence of illness and suffering at many different levels, far beyond what my family and I are experiencing right now. These examples certainly display the temporal consequences of sin.

Sinfulness has also brought self-centeredness rather than God-centeredness. The Scriptures are rife with examples of this from the blame shifting of Adam and Eve in Genesis 3, the first murder when Cain kills Abel, the illicit sexual sins throughout the rest of the Pentateuch, the sins of other nations against Israel, and the sins of Israel against their covenant God. The latter of these sins we see God bring the consequences of Israel's sin against Him by bringing

---

14. Berkhof, *Systematic Theology*, 256.

those sinful outside nations to capture Israel to make them aware of their sin against Him.

We must also acknowledge the eternal consequences of sin, which are seen in the very first command of God that if Adam and Eve disobey God, they "will certainly die" (Gen. 3:17). This death is both physical and spiritual. If one is not saved from this consequence, it equals eternal death. There is no turning back from this ultimate consequence. As we stated previously, this is what is right and just from a Holy God. Indeed, God "saves" Adam and Eve from this consequence by slaughtering an animal to cover their sin when He "made clothing from skins for the man and his wife" (Gen. 3:21). This ultimate consequence is the gravest of all for mankind's sin. Sin has infected every aspect of not only who mankind is, but also the very creation itself. We recall from the events of the early chapters of Genesis that mankind faces the curse of sin, but so does creation. God tells Adam that he will have to cultivate the earth under the curse of sin. What was delightful worshipful dominion, will now be grueling work under the fall (Gen. 3).

Romans 8:20 describes creation as "subjected to futility" because of mankind's sin. As we shall see, this is not a surprise to God somehow, but rather, as we have described God as other than us, He is working even this together for His own glory (Rom. 8:28). But for now, we must see that this subjection to futility has come about because of mankind's rebellion. The fruit of this is seen not only throughout Scripture, but also throughout human history. The decay of mankind and creation is intertwined because of sin. Not only is mankind's labor more intense because of the fall, the creation itself was changed in order to accommodate this intensified labor. Where there was more easily tilled earth before the fall, there is now harder ground to cultivate. Where there was no obstruction to growing God's abundant plant life, now there are thorns and thistles. The dwelling place of God and man is no longer what it was and indeed mankind is cast out of the garden—the place once meant for mankind and God to dwell together. Indeed, mankind and creation seem to be at odds as well. We see the destruction of mankind at the hand of nature in every tornado that destroys a town and takes lives, every tsunami that surges beyond the coast and washes away entire villages. We can even see evidence of this on a smaller scale, like my constant battle with trying to keep water out of my basement in the rainy seasons. All these realities that we face post-fall are a result of the sinfulness of mankind in the garden.

Additionally, we see that mankind is barred from the garden specifically so that he will not have access to the tree of life. God says in Genesis 3:22–24:

"Since the man has become like one of us, knowing good and evil, he must not reach out, take from the tree of life, eat, and live forever." So the LORD God sent him away from the garden of Eden to work the ground from which he was taken. He drove the man out and stationed the cherubim and the flaming, whirling sword east of the garden of Eden to guard the way to the tree of life.

In summary, what was once a place of dwelling for God and mankind is no longer; what was once an opportunity for mankind to obey and fill the earth and subdue it is now a place of blood, sweat, and tears. What was once a promise of eternal life is no longer accessible to mankind. There was a need for someone else to come and obey where Adam disobeyed. This promise is also found in Genesis 3.

The *Protoevangelium* and the Hope of Glorification

Even in the midst of these great curses, there is also a curse upon the serpent through whom the devil deceived mankind. But amid the curse upon the serpent is a promise of hope that God makes to mankind as well. As you may know, in Genesis 3:15 the Lord says to the serpent, "I will put hostility between you and the woman, and between your offspring and her offspring. He will strike your head, and you will strike his heel." Theologians have coined this the *protoevangelium* or the first gospel. The plight of every childbearing woman is greater pain associated with childbirth than what would have been before the fall. However, it is exactly childbirth that will bring about the salvation from the very effects of the fall, that which God will provide through the woman's seed.

It may seem like this promise God makes to Adam and Eve doesn't have anything to do with glorification. It, however, has everything to do with it. The promise that a man (the offspring or seed of Gen. 3:15) will strike the head of the serpent, is the gospel in seed form. As Geerhardus Vos says, "The first redemptive revelation after the fall had this [objective eschatological] element in it, because it predicted the final victory over sin, the removal of the curse, and, by implication, the return of the conditions of paradise."[15] As I have argued previously, Vos does not see "the return to the conditions of paradise" as the ultimate hope, but rather agrees that "the symbol of the tree of life [holds] out the

---

15. Geerhardus Vos, *The Eschatology of the Old Testament* (Philipsburg, NJ: P&R Publishing, 2001), 37.

prospect of a higher life," and we could say a glorified life.[16] Throughout the rest of the Pentateuch (the first five books of the Bible) God's promise continues to flower into something greater yet. We see hints of this in places like Genesis 49 and Deuteronomy 18 where pictures of a king reigning and a prophet rising colors the way for the Old Testament people of God that leads to the prophets expecting a coming Messiah who would fulfill the promise of Genesis 3:15. One cannot help but have the new covenant promises of Jeremiah and Ezekiel come to mind where God promises:

> "Look, the days are coming"—this is the LORD's declaration—"when I will make a new covenant with the house of Israel and with the house of Judah. This one will not be like the covenant I made with their ancestors on the day I took them by the hand to lead them out of the land of Egypt—my covenant that they broke even though I am their master"—the LORD's declaration. "Instead, this is the covenant I will make with the house of Israel after those days"—the LORD's declaration. "I will put my teaching within them and write it on their hearts. I will be their

---

16. Vos, *The Eschatology of the Old Testament*, 37.

God, and they will be my people. No longer will one teach his neighbor or his brother, saying, 'Know the LORD,' for they will all know me, from the least to the greatest of them"—this is the LORD's declaration. "For I will forgive their iniquity and never again remember their sin." (Jer. 31:31–34)

And "I will give you a new heart and put a new spirit within you; I will remove your heart of stone and give you a heart of flesh. I will place my Spirit within you and cause you to follow my statutes and carefully observe my ordinances" (Ezek. 36:26–27).

This truth is captured supremely by the prophet Isaiah by whom God grants us access to the realities of the coming kingdom of God in which we will dwell in glory; from the suffering servant of Isaiah 53 to the promise of a new heaven and earth in Isaiah 65. Further we see the New Testament fulfillment of Messiah in Jesus Christ and the hope of glory in and through His perfect life, death, and resurrection and the promise of His return subsequent to His ascension.

Conclusion

This chapter highlights the fall from glory in which, through mankind's disobedience, the promise of what could have been a glorious existence is exchanged for a miserable existence. We have outlined that sin is failing to reach the goal of God's glorious standard and that we should expect nothing less since we are descendants of Adam who was the first to transgress God's law. Though through their sinning Adam and Eve plunge humanity and creation into a miserable state, God also makes a gospel promise amid the curse in which there will be one who comes that will crush the head of the serpent though the serpent will bruise His heal. All these truths, beginning in the garden, point to the restored hope of glory as is seen in the incarnational work of the Lord Jesus Christ, to which we turn next.

RESTORED TO THE
HOPE OF GLORY

*"All religions seek a way of salvation; all
human being long for happiness because
the human heart is created for God."*[1]
—Herman Bavinck

The quote from Herman Bavinck, the great nineteenth-
and twentieth-century Dutch Reformed theologian,
echoes the words of wise King Solomon who says that God
"has put eternity in" the "hearts" of the "children of Adam"
(Eccles. 3:9–11). There is no escaping eternity or the eternal
triune God. Because mankind fell into sin and separated
himself from a right relationship with God, he has also

---

1. Herman Bavinck, *Reformed Dogmatics*, vol. 3 (Grand Rapids: Baker
Academic, 2006), 485.

found other ways to fill the longing for happiness and thus forged a new way of "salvation."

A longing for eternity in the hearts of men seems to drive this new way of "salvation." What mankind seeks is a rest that only comes through God and His saving work. However, as I discussed in our last chapter, mankind fell from God's glorious purpose for them, and this fall not only brings mankind into a sinful state, but creation as well. The greatest part of this fall, though, is the severing of mankind from a right relationship with the triune God. It is the end goal of the triune God to bring those whom He has redeemed into His rest, His very presence, experiencing the vision of God. This goal of rest is seen even in the beginning and yet was forfeited through mankind's sin. But God, in His goodness and eternal decree, saw fit to bring about not only the justification of mankind through reconciling them to Himself through Christ, but also to sanctify them, making them into the image of Christ through union with Him, until that rest is final in glorification where they will dwell with Him in all His glorious beauty.

The way in which God accomplishes this is through the life, death, and resurrection of Christ, which is the centerpiece of Christian hope for salvation. The triune God in His great grace and mercy set out a plan before time began for the redemption of a people for Himself (Eph. 1:3–14; 2:1–10;

Titus 2:14). Without Christ's perfect life (active obedience), death (passive obedience), and resurrection, we would have no salvation from God's justice or reconciliation to Him. In summary, as Paul exclaims to Timothy, "This saying is trustworthy and deserving of full acceptance: 'Christ Jesus came into the world to save sinners'" (1 Tim. 1:15). The finished work of Christ, this cornerstone of our faith, is the foundation of our union with Christ and we need to look further at its importance.

Growing up, I remember hearing many sermons about being saved from hell. Very little if any emphasis was placed upon our union with Christ. Granted, the reality of hell is certainly a motivation for trusting Christ, but to what end? The tradition had a very earthly-oriented view of eternal life. This may seem contradictory, but heaven was more about an alternative destiny to hell rather than an understanding of union with Christ in His life, death, and resurrection. Eternal life was something obtained but not really explained. Therefore, I was not given the hope of Christ's finished work as how I would be reconciled to God to enjoy His glory forever. Don't get me wrong, my pastors and leaders were certainly concerned about getting the gospel right, and they did teach salvation by grace alone through faith alone. However, I never heard that "man's chief end is to glorify God, and to enjoy Him forever."[2] Whether it was me growing up without such knowledge or those who only know of God's existence through His natural revelation, what we come to understand is that mankind is without hope in this world, but for God.

As we have already discussed, the apostle Paul writes about these truths to the church in Rome and explains that because mankind refuses to acknowledge God, even though they know He exists, they determine to make their own religion by worshipping the creation rather than the Creator (Rom. 1). Paul is also quick to point out that even though Israel has been granted the oracles and promises of God, they are not able to escape the consequences of sin, for all have fallen short of God's glorious standard (Rom. 1-3). That consequence is made clear when Paul later writes that the wages of sin is death, but hope arises when he further states that the gift of God is eternal life through Jesus Christ our Lord (Rom. 6:23). Ah! There is the relief for which all mankind longs. Not only do they long for the relief from sin, but also to be in the presence of God seeing Him in all His beauty (Ps. 27:4). This part of our study is the point where things take a turn and set us on a trajectory for why we have the hope of glorification.

---

2. Westminster Shorter Catechism, Q1.

This turn takes us back to an earlier part of our discussion where we look at the three parts of the whole of our salvation, namely: justification, sanctification, and glorification. When we, by God's grace, realize our sinfulness, it is also by God's grace that He grants us repentance and faith. Repentance implies a turning away from one's sin, and faith implies a turning to Christ. In one sense we are turning from one object to another object. To use the words of Paul in Romans 1, we are turning from worship of creature to Creator. It is exemplified in the testimony of the Thessalonian saints where Paul rejoices that they "turned to God from idols to serve the living and true God and to wait for his Son from heaven, whom he raised from the dead—Jesus, who rescues us from the coming wrath" (1 Thess. 1:9–10). The Thessalonian church was transformed by justification through faith in Christ. They became worshippers of the true and living God. Again, whether we worship the God of the Bible or one of our own making, worship is inherent in all humanity.

Just as there was a sense of worship in the garden of Eden, we do not cease to worship after the fall. Mankind is prone to worship and therefore, if we are false, we worship what is false and vice versa. As Psalm 115:8 states, "Those who make [idols] are just like them." Greg Beale summarizes this well in the title of his book *We Become What We Worship.*

He is not suggesting that becoming what we worship is a physical reality, but rather a metaphorical idea that speaks of the heart of those who worship false gods—which is all unregenerate humanity (Rom. 1:18–23). One of my favorite depictions of this metaphor is when Beale points out that Israel has become stiff-necked like the golden calf that they worship in Exodus 32. Beale states, "The first generation Israelites did not literally become petrified gold calves like the golden calf they worshiped, but they are depicted as acting like out-of-control and headstrong calves apparently because they are being mocked as having become identified with the spiritually rebellious image of the calf that they had worshiped."[3] If this is true for the unregenerate, in what sense does the believer properly worship the triune God and what does this have to do with our glorification?

First, it takes a regenerated heart to have our sights turned back to God, and this new heart is the beginning of a restoration of sorts, but with an aim toward that which is greater. Some say that the redeemed are headed back to an Edenic reality. But as I state above, Eden was only the beginning. Mankind was heading toward something greater. If in Adam all die, and in Christ all who are in Him are made righteous, this means something concerning the future of

---

3. Greg Beale, *We Become What We Worship: A Biblical Theology of Idolatry* (Downers Grove, IL: InterVarsity, 2008), 82.

humanity. One whose heart is turned back to proper worship of God is also set on a trajectory toward a truer humanity that is found in the humanity of Christ. Second, we can see how being made in the image of Christ and indeed being glorified as He is, counters the idea of becoming like the false gods that humanity worships. Considering these things, we must turn to the idea of union with Christ.

Union with Christ

We will see that just as mankind is represented by Adam, we all find ourselves sinners, so too those who are in Christ are represented by Him and are in union with Him. The Scriptures are clear about this representative reality. Once again, we appeal to Paul in Romans who by the Holy Spirit helps us understand this truth. Romans 5:12–21 frames our understanding. Since it is a rather long passage to simply place amid our text here, I will break it down into two concepts that I will support with scriptural references.

Through One Man Sin Entered the World

As we stated earlier in our study, mankind was plunged into sinfulness by being represented by Adam (Rom. 5:12). The reality of sin entering the world is not because the law highlights it, but rather the consequence of sin is upon all men, that is, all men die. In other words, the evidence of sinfulness is that all men die. Paul's argument is that death was inevitable even before the Mosaic law. To think on the opposite, it seems to prove what we argued earlier that without sin, mankind would have at least continued to live on in innocence, if not also through obedience have earned an escalation to everlasting life. In this sense, we can see how Adam was a type of the one to come, as Paul says. The way in which we ought to understand this is that Adam is a representative of humanity. This construct is known as federal theology. Federal theology maintains that Adam legally represents all of humanity in his obedience or disobedience.[4] The federal headship of Adam reflects what we argue concerning the outcome of Adam's obedience or his sin. Whatever Adam chose results in what mankind becomes. Since Adam chose to disobey God, the entire human race is united with him in that disobedience. When Adam sinned, he forfeited the garden, a right relationship with God, a right relationship with his wife, an easier cultivation of the

---

4. Federal theology suggests that as the first human, Adam acted as the "federal head" (from Latin *foedus*, "covenant") or legal representative of the rest of humankind. Thus God entered into a covenantal relationship with Adam that promised blessing for obedience and a curse for disobedience. Stanley Grenz, David Guretzki, and Cherith Fee Nordling, *Pocket Dictionary of Theological Terms* (Downers Grove, IL: InterVarsity, 1999), 50–51.

earth, etc. We are all united with him in that. Had Adam succeeded his probationary period we would have been untied with him in that. However, He did not and so we were united with him in his death. God tells Adam and Eve that if they disobey Him, they will surely die (Gen. 2:17). That death was not immediate in a physical sense, but I believe we can rightly state it is immediate in a spiritual sense to be followed by the physical sense. To put it bluntly like Paul does in 1 Corinthians 15:22, "in Adam all die."

Through One Man Many Will Be Made Righteous

Paul states that just as through one man all have been made sinners, through one man (the God-Man) many will be made righteous. This is not a righteousness of our own design, but that which is won for us by Christ. He lived the perfect life we could not, died the death that we deserved, and rose again. We are now clothed with the righteousness of Christ and declared righteous because of His finished work. This is what happens when we are justified.

Because those who are in Christ are federally represented by Him, they are new creations—the old has passed, the new has come (2 Cor. 5:17). This newness is not just a reality of the here and now but is a breaking in of the newness that is to come in the new heaven and earth. We have a fore-taste of glory divine, as the old hymn says.[5] The "already" of the reality of being united with Christ is as Paul states to the Ephesian church that we are "no longer children of wrath, but we are saved by grace!" (Eph. 2:5). Beyond this "already" reality Paul also states, "He also raised us up with him and seated us with him in the heavens in Christ Jesus" (2:6). Notice the present tense here points our "already" being seated with Christ in the heavens. Here we come to an *already* reality of the kingdom breaking into the here and now. As Samuel Renihan expresses, "The people of the church . . . are the people of the new creation. They are a new humanity in the second and last Adam."[6] Those who are united to Christ will be united to Him now and forever-more, which brings hope now as God fulfills His promises in Christ and as He has given us a down payment in the giving of His Spirit. Paul, earlier in the same passage we have been examining in Ephesians says, "In him you also were sealed with the promised Holy Spirit when you heard the word of truth, the gospel of your salvation, and when you believed. The Holy Spirit is the down payment of our inheritance,

---

5. Fanny Crosby, "Blessed Assurance," public domain.
6. Samuel Renihan, *The Mystery of Christ, His Covenant, and His Kingdom* (Cape Coral, FL: Founders Press, 2020), 196.

until the redemption of the possession, to the praise of his glory" (Eph. 1:13–14).

Union with Christ in Justification: Imputed Righteousness

In Romans, we see Paul's unequivocal language concerning justification that even as mankind has "fallen short of God's glory," any who believe "are justified by his grace as a gift, through the redemption that is in Jesus Christ" (Rom. 3:23–24). The word *justified* is generally understood as one "being acquitted . . . and treated as righteous."[7]

The scriptural idea at which we are aiming is that if we hold to union with Christ as an "imputational" theology, the work is already accomplished. Federal theology speaks of two imputations: all humanity as fallen in Adam, imputed with his sin, and believers united to Christ imputed with His righteousness. This understanding of imputation is what the Bible itself demonstrates in Romans 5:12 and 1 Corinthians 15:22. Michael Horton submits, "The Reformers . . . focus on union with Christ and see this union as the source rather than the goal of final salvation. This goal [is] . . . the whole self-united *now* to the whole Christ and, through him, to

---

7. S.v., "δικαιόω," BDAG.

the Father."[8] Again, we speak of this union in terms of the righteousness of Christ imputed to the believer. This imputation of righteousness carries the idea of transmission. Vos describes it as "transferring to [one] the objective relationship of righteousness from someone else."[9] This concept of righteousness as coming from outside of the person from someone else is called an "alien righteousness." That is, it is not a righteousness that is resident within them that must be awakened, but rather a righteousness that is reckoned to them from someone else who has the claim of being righteous. Therefore, the active obedience of Christ plays a crucial role in our understanding of justification. When it comes to the believer's right standing before the holy triune God, it is not due to anything they have outside of being found in Christ and the gift of His perfections, His righteousness. Highlighting the continuity between union with Christ, imputation, and federal representation, Turretin writes:

> Christ by his obedience is rightly said "to
> constitute" us "righteous" not by inherent
> but by an imputed righteousness as taught
> in Romans 4:6 teaches and gathered from

---

8. Michael Horton, *Justification*, vol. *1*, ed. Michael Allen and Scott R. Swain (Grand Rapids: Zondervan Academic, 2018), 200. Emphasis mine.
9. Geerhardus Vos, *Reformed Dogmatics*, vol. 4, ed. Richard B. Gaffin Jr., trans. Richard B. Gaffin Jr. (Bellingham: Lexham Press, 2012–2016), 137.

the opposition of the antecedent opposition (Rom. 5:19). For they are no less constituted righteous before God who, on account of the obedience of Christ imputed to them, are absolved from deserved punishment, than they who on account of the disobedience of Adam are constituted as unrighteous. . . . If Adam constituted us unrighteous effectively by the propagation of inherent depravity (on account of which we were also exposed to death in the sight of God), it does not follow equally that Christ constitutes us righteous by a forensic justification at the bar of God by inherent righteousness given to us by him.[10]

What Turretin expresses here is the representative language we outline above. Humanity in union with Adam and his sin become inherently sinners. Those who come to faith in Christ are united to Him and His perfect work and have His righteousness credited to their account.

Considering the already/not yet paradigm, justification, as put forth here, fits squarely in the realm of the "already."

---

10. Francis Turretin, *Institutes of Elenctic Theology, Vol. 2: Eleventh Through Seventeenth Topics,* ed. James T. Dennison Jr., trans. George Musgrave Giger (Phillipsburg, NJ: P&R Publishing, 1992), 644.

However, this is but one facet of the believer's union with Christ in the realm of salvation. We will investigate the believer's union with Christ in their sanctification in chapter 6. For now, it is important for us to examine the glorification aspect of our current chapter. We will do this by examining our union with Christ in the beatific vision.

Union with Christ and the Beatific Vision

Our union with Christ, though a reality now, is not fully realized until we see Him as He is. The apostle John in his first epistle makes this hope known to us. He tells us, "Dear friends, we are God's children now, and what we will be has not yet been revealed. We know that when he appears, we will be like him because we will see him as he is" (1 John 3:2). The hope set forth in this chapter is again one that entails the already/not yet. We are already the children of God. The assurance of our union with Christ is sure. We are currently counted among the children of God, the adopted ones who are in the family of God (Eph. 1). However, there are aspects of this reality that are grounded in heaven. Paul states that we have all these riches already set in the heavenly places where Christ is currently seated and reigning with God (Eph. 1). However, the full realization of this union is not obtained until He appears. This appearing is what I described earlier as the beatific vision or the *visio Dei* (the vision of God). As I said earlier, you may associate such language with Roman Catholicism or Eastern Orthodoxy, or other high church settings. However, I assure you that many over the centuries, including those from the Reformed tradition have spoken positively of the beatific vision. John Calvin states thusly:

> Because the fervor of desire must be kindled in us by some taste of its sweetness, let us specially dwell upon this thought, If God contains in himself as an inexhaustible fountain all fullness of blessing, those who aspire to the supreme good and perfect happiness must not long for any thing beyond him. . . . If our Lord will share his glory, power, and righteousness, with the elect, nay, will give himself to be enjoyed by them; and what is better still, will, in a manner, become one with them, let us remember that every kind of happiness is herein included.[11]

---

11. John Calvin, *Institutes of the Christian Religion*, 3.25.10.

Though Calvin does not directly use the term "beatific vision" here, per se, the clear implication of this quote is that in the future believers will obtain a special union with God in Christ by the Spirit that exceeds what we experience currently. While we do not have space here to explore all the details of the beatific vision, it is important to highlight what it has to do with our union with Christ ultimately. It is the ultimate way in which we will glorify God and enjoy Him forever. It is to say by virtue of our union with Christ we experience true communion with God in eternity.

Conclusion

As we conclude this chapter, an illustration comes to mind from the Old Testament. If you're a Christian, you're probably familiar with the events surrounding the Tower of Babel. The people who band together to create this city do so to seek a name for themselves (Gen. 11:4). Rather than making a name for God their Creator, they seek glory for themselves. Instead of seeking God's grace for a celestial city, they seek to build their own. Instead of seeking God's face in the prescribed way, they seek to build a tower that reaches to Him. The pride of mankind from the garden to the Tower of Babel and beyond. The restoration to a hope of glory is wrapped up in God's glorious gospel. If chapter 4 describes the bad news of mankind's fall from glory, this chapter expresses the good news of God's grace and mercy toward sinners.

THE PROMISE
OF GLORY

"By God's final judgment, which shall be
administered by His Son Jesus Christ, there
shall by God's grace be manifested a glory so
pervading and so new, that no vestige of what
is old shall remain; for even our bodies shall
pass from their old corruption and mortality
to new incorruption and immortality."[1]
—St. Augustine of Hippo

Augustine is probably the most famous church father. Even those who have little knowledge of church history have usually heard of his work, the *City of God*. In the

_____

1. Augustine of Hippo, "The City of God," in *St. Augustin's City of God and Christian Doctrine*, vol. 2, ed. Philip Schaff, trans. Marcus Dods, A Select Library of the Nicene and Post-Nicene Fathers of the Christian Church, First Series (Buffalo, NY: Christian Literature Company, 1887), 436.

above quote, Augustine details a good bit of his theological work starting with an apologetic for the one true God and transitioning to the two cities and their beginnings, development, and consummation.[2] We find, in the quote above, an expression of the consummation of both the created order and mankind.

What Augustine captures in this quote and its surrounding context is not just the consummation, but the environment of it. It is the descending of the heavenly city upon the earthly city in the atmosphere of God's unveiled glory. The glory of the church in the new heaven and new earth reflects the glory of God. The passage which spurs these comments from Augustine is Revelation 21:1-5, which reads:

> Then I saw a new heaven and a new earth; for the first heaven and the first earth had passed away, and the sea was no more. I also saw the holy city, the new Jerusalem, coming down out of heaven from God, prepared like a bride adorned for her husband.
>
> Then I heard a loud voice from the throne: Look, God's dwelling is with humanity, and he will live with them. They will be his peoples, and God himself will be with

---

2. The two cities being the City of God and the City of Man.

them and will be their God. He will wipe
away every tear from their eyes. Death will
be no more; grief, crying, and pain will be
no more, because the previous things have
passed away.

Then the one seated on the throne said,
"Look, I am making everything new."

In the last chapter we worked through what it means
to be in union with Christ and how this makes the believer
ready in this life for the next. That is, as we said, we are justified and are being sanctified progressively all toward the
end of our glorification. As we begin this chapter we will
explore how when at the time of the consummation of all
things we will be made whole according to our new nature;
the already becoming the not yet. Considering the passage
above we are contemplating with the Scriptures, Augustine,
and others what it means that heaven comes down to earth,
and that God's dwelling is now with humanity.

We notice first that a new heaven and new earth are
in view and first heaven and earth pass away. This sort of
cosmological language sets up a parenthetical statement
in these verses; the old has passed away and God is making everything new. There are details that we need to trace
out together. But first, I want us to recognize this paradigm
of old and new. It is reminiscent of the believer in this life.

As Paul tells us, "Therefore, if anyone is in Christ, he is a new creation; the old has passed away, and see, the new has come!" (2 Cor. 5:17). This verse emphasizes what we have said previously that there is an already/not yet aspect of consummation that is realized in the experience of the believer before the consummation even occurs. Here we see the parallel of this reality in the universe's consummation as well. As with the believer who has a down payment for glorification in the future, so too does creation, who awaits with anticipation this reality as Paul states in Romans 8:21: "Creation itself will also be set free from the bondage to decay into the glorious freedom of God's children."

And lest we miss the point of John's vision here, as Greg Beale states, "The part of the new creation that John focuses on is the redeemed saints. The vision in John 21:2–22:5 is thus dominated by various figurative portrayals of the glorified community of believers."[3] Even as with the beginning of the world this new creation is meant to dwell with God, though as we have argued, with an escalated feature that was not yet present in the garden.

Indeed, the focus is upon God dwelling with men. It is due to the nature of mankind being prepared for eternity

---

3. G. K. Beale, *The Book of Revelation: A Commentary on the Greek Text*, New International Greek Testament Commentary (Grand Rapids: Eerdmans, 1999), 1041.

with God. The effects of sin are no longer a hinderance of God living with His people. Notice what John says, "He will wipe away every tear from their eyes. Death will be no more; grief, crying, and pain will be no more, because the previous things have passed away" (21:4). There is a sense in which sin is seen as outside the believer here, though in their sinfulness certainly believers have perpetrated grievous things upon one another that have caused grief, crying, and pain. In this new environment, however, there is no way in which these elements will be present. Indeed, death, the culminating effect of sin, will be no more. Of course, we have seen in previous passages that this condemnation of death is forecasted at the cross where Christ has defeated death and the grave (Isa. 25:8; Hosea 13:14; 1 Cor. 15:54–55). The overwhelming sense of this passage is the hope to which we are discussing in this book. We can hardly imagine these realities because we deal with the grief associated with our own sin and the sins of others against us. However, for the believer there is a confident certainty that these promises will come to pass. The gospel of Jesus Christ comforts us in this life, but not only as those who have been forgiven and united to Christ, but because of His work, we know that these prophetic words will one day be our reality. It is now our goal to press into the coming reality of resurrection life.

Resurrection Life

Paul proclaims in 1 Corinthians 15:49 that "just as we have borne the image of the man of dust, we will also bear the image of the man of heaven." We showed previously that there is a union with Adam in the fall and that once a person comes to faith in Christ there is a union with Christ. Here we come to that union concerning the resurrection. Paul makes clear that we will bear the image of Christ in His resurrection when he further states:

> Flesh and blood cannot inherit the kingdom
> of God, nor can corruption inherit incorrup-
> tion. Listen, I am telling you a mystery: We will
> not all fall asleep, but we will all be changed,
> in a moment, in the twinkling of an eye, at
> the last trumpet. For the trumpet will sound,
> and the dead will be raised incorruptible,
> and we will be changed. For this corruptible
> body must be clothed with incorruptibility,
> and this mortal body must be clothed with
> immortality. (1 Cor. 15:50–53)

We note in summary that we will change from our corruptible bodies into immortal bodies. This change will occur at the resurrection, either when our dead bodies rise to meet with Jesus or if we are living during His return at the same meeting (1 Thess. 4:16–17). The apostle John, who we have referenced, says that when we see Him, we will be like Him (1 John 3:2). This hope is not just found in one place but is sprinkled throughout Scripture.

Describing Resurrection Life

We need to spend some time describing what this resurrection life will be like, at least as much as we can gather from Scripture and contemplate it along with those who have gone before us. In the same passage we reference above, Paul describes the differences between the body that dies and the one that is transformed through resurrection, stating, "it is . . . sown in corruption, raised in incorruption; sown in dishonor, raised in glory; sown in weakness, raised in power; sown a natural body, raised a spiritual body" (1 Cor. 15:42–44). Let's take each of these comparisons and work them out a bit.[4]

---

4. Though I do not directly quote Francis Turretin in this section, he similarly works through this passage in his "Last Things" section under the Ninth Question: What are the endowments and qualities of glorified bodies? See Francis Turretin, *Institutes of Elenctic Theology, Vol. 3: Eighteenth Through Twentieth Topics*, ed. James T. Dennison Jr. (Phillipsburg, NJ: P&R Publishing, 1997), 617–21.

Sown in corruption, raised in incorruption

We know that our bodies are corruptible. The older I get the more I experience this reality. One of Shakespeare's most famous plays is *The Merchant of Venice*, which also contains one of the most famous lines in all of theater. Spoken by Shylock, the antagonist of the play, who in making an argument for human equality says, "If you prick us, do we not bleed? If you tickle us, do we not laugh? If you poison us, do we not die?"[5] While we may find it hard to agree with Shylock's character and motives, his questions do help us see humanity's mortality. When we speak of corruption, we are not speaking of the wicked actions of men (though we cannot disconnect the reality of sin's activity and its effects). Instead, we are speaking of the decay we all face. Our bodies are breaking down. Paul again addresses this in the Scriptures when he says, "Even though our outer person is being destroyed, our inner person is being renewed day by day" (2 Cor. 4:16). Though this passage nods to sanctification, the day-by-day renewal of our inner person, Paul then goes on to speak of our bodies as tents that are being destroyed in the very next passage. He describes us as groaning in these bodies as we await our heavenly dwelling. Our minds may immediately think of dwelling here as the

---

5. William Shakespeare, *The Merchant of Venice*, Act 3, Scene 1.

entire dwelling place (the new heaven and new earth), but instead Paul is very specifically referencing our bodies, for he goes on to say that we want to be clothed so that "mortality may be swallowed up by life." Further he links sanctification to glorification by saying, "Now the one who prepared us for this very purpose is God, who gave us the Spirit as a down payment" (2 Cor. 5:5).[6]

The next phrase, "raised in incorruption," is exactly what Paul is referring to when he speaks of the heavenly dwelling as we just saw. The reality of the transformation of the resurrection is that believers will no longer have corruptible bodies. Our bodies will be fit for eternity. As Paul says:

> Flesh and blood cannot inherit the kingdom of God, nor can corruption inherit incorruption. Listen, I am telling you a mystery: We will not all fall asleep, but we will all be changed, in a moment, in the twinkling of an eye, at the last trumpet. For the trumpet will sound, and the dead will be raised incorruptible, and we will be changed. For this corruptible body must be clothed

---

6. We will see in our next chapter how exactly sanctification is linked to glorification, but for now we see evidence here from Paul.

with incorruptibility, and this mortal body must be clothed with immortality. (1 Cor. 15:50–53)

Notice that Paul says the dead will be raised incorruptible and we will be changed. There are two categories of people that Paul refers to in 1 Thessalonians 4, when he says the dead in Christ will rise first and then we who are alive will meet Jesus in the air. Both categories of the redeemed—both the dead and the living—will be changed from corruptible to incorruptible. The decay brought about by the fall will be reversed. Though many use the phrase "new bodies," we agree with Calvin that these bodies will not be new but transformed and "invested with glory."[7] And as Turretin emphasizes, it is also true with Christ that He had the same body.[8] It is our union with Christ that guarantees us the same as we see in Philippians 3:21, "He will transform the body of our humble condition into the likeness of his glorious body." Further, Turretin expresses that the immortality of the saints is "by grace from the beatific vision of God."[9] Once again,

---

7. John Calvin and John Pringle, *Commentaries on the Epistles of Paul the Apostle to the Corinthians*, vol. 2 (Bellingham, WA: Logos Bible Software, 2010), 61.
8. Turretin, *Institutes of Elenctic Theology*, 3:573.
9. Turretin, *Institutes of Elenctic Theology*, 3:618.

1 John 3:2 points us to this reality "that when he appears, we will be like him because we will see him as he is."

Sown in dishonor, raised in glory

We understand the idea of sown as the burial of the body of the person who has died. Dishonor does not mean that the person was buried in a less than honorable way. Rather it is the condition of fallenness in which the person died. Gill remarks that the dead body is "nauseous, filthy, and very dishonourable, so that the nearest relation and friend cannot take pleasure in it, but desires to bury it out of sight; and amidst the greatest funereal pomp and splendour, it is laid in the grave in dishonour, to be the companion of corruption and worms."[10]

The true Christian has been brought from death to life. Once again, there is an *already* aspect to this and yet a *not yet* that will result in the fullness of glorification. To the point, the believer who dies is buried in the fallen body but raised in a glorified body. Bringing back an earlier part of our study, the believer is justified (declared righteous) at a point in time and then is sanctified (made more holy, more like Jesus) throughout their life, but is still awaiting the fullness of their salvation when body and soul will both be

10. John Gill, *An Exposition of the New Testament*, vol. 2, The Baptist Commentary Series (London: Mathews and Leigh, 1809), 741.

redeemed. A point that this truth raises in addition to what is mentioned in the previous section is that the body is not evil. This is a gnostic idea that the apostle John refutes. John, on the one hand speaks of the necessity of Jesus having flesh to be truly human we "have touched" (1 John 1:1) but does not deny the reality of the flesh's need to be redeemed, the lust of the flesh (v. 9). He also contrasts God as light and that those who walk in darkness cannot be in the light, but that those who are in Christ are in the light, and are denying the lust of the flesh and the eyes and the boastful pride of life, meaning that mankind is flesh and soul and those who are redeemed will be changed, but will still struggle with a flesh that needs to be redeemed. Therefore, the flesh is not evil, but it needs to be redeemed. Therefore, when we think of our bodies being sown in dishonor, and subsequently raised in glory, we should think of the need of the transformation of the body to a glorified state as well.

Sown in weakness, raised in power

The weakness of the corruptible body seems obvious; the body is given to decay. Humanity, regardless of spiritual life or death, will bodily breakdown. There is an entire industry built around health and wellness because we recognize that our bodies grow weaker—in various ways—over time. We have all heard the stories of the healthy marathon runner who disciplined his body through diet and exercise, but suddenly dies of a heart attack. What is the typical response to this sort of scenario? "He was the model of health!" Of course, we would not say as the epicureans "eat drink and be merry for tomorrow we die!" No, we would applaud healthy life decisions, but with Paul we would agree that it is of little value in the scope of eternity (1 Tim. 4:8), and certainly he does not say it has no value. The point is, however, that our bodies are weak. We may also think of it in line with the fall and the curse of the ground that mankind will labor with less control over the earth due to the fall. In the grand scheme of things, what is a bee sting as compared to a tornado? We can easily get over a bee sting, unless, of course, the person has a life-threatening allergy, but there is a greater likelihood that a person will not stand strong against the tornado. The fall has weakened our bodies.

However, when it comes to glorification, while we will certainly experience the pre-fall existence of sin, we should understand the glorification of the body as something greater than even Adam experienced. Though we may not be able to conceive of exactly what that means, it at least implies that sin will not be capable of weakening the glorified body. Here again we come back to the idea that the entrance of sin will be impossible in the glorified state.

Sown a natural body, raised a spiritual body

Paul's description here may be the most mysterious for us. Our minds may immediately rush to the question "What is a spiritual body?" And we would not be out of line since Paul mentions this concept twice within the same breath. He employs this final description more firmly stating, "if there is a natural body, there is also a spiritual body." Paul once again draws the imperfect parallel of Adam and Christ when he states, "The first man Adam became a living being; the last Adam became a life-giving spirit" (1 Cor. 15:44–45). Paul gives us insight in another passage we previously referenced, Romans 7:24–25. Earlier in this passage Paul speaks of the struggle between the inner man that loves God's law and the flesh that still needs to be redeemed. As you read it, you sense Paul's frustration as he doesn't always do the things he wants to do and sometimes does the things he doesn't want to do. The frustration reaches its apex when Paul cries out with the question of who will free him from this body of death. His reply is that this relief will come finally through Jesus Christ.

Of this portion Augustine says, "For as, when the spirit serves the flesh, it is fitly called carnal, so, when the flesh serves the spirit, it will justly be called spiritual. Not that it is converted into spirit . . . but because it is subject to the spirit with a perfect and marvelous readiness of obedience, and responds in all things to the will that has entered on immortality—all reluctance, all corruption, and all slowness being removed."[11]

Fit for Eternity

Lest we fall into the trap of which I have heard Christians speak my entire church life, let's be clear that the goal of the resurrection and glorification is not our sinless, painless existence, but rather the triune God and communion with Him for which we will be fitted for existence. The true treasure of our eternal existence is God Himself but we still must be made ready for this existence through glorification.

Recall when Moses asked God to see His glory that God said to him, "You cannot see my face, for humans cannot see me and live" (Exod. 33:20). Even though Moses was one who "talked with God face to face," and in this sense Moses spoke with God as a friend, Moses was still not allowed to see God's glory because it would kill him. So God passes by Moses while He has him hidden in a rock so that Moses heard God's glorious statement concerning himself and Moses only got a glimpse of the tail end of God's glory. This

---

11. Augustine, *City of God*, 255–56.

tiny glimpse was all that Moses could see and not die. But when God himself puts on humanity and veils the glory of a season, John says that we have seen His glory (John 1:14) and that the incarnate Son of God reveals (exegetes) the triune God to us (John 1:18). In our fallenness we need a veiled glory.

However, in our resurrected and glorified state, we will see God. Earlier we spoke of the beatific vision, the blessed sight of God in His glory, as it has been said, we shall see the glory of God in the face of Jesus Christ (1 John 3:2). It is impossible for us in our current fallen bodies to exist in the fullness of God's glorious presence. As Sam Parkison states this reality "will be enjoyed in a consummated way in the beatific vision on the other side of the resurrection."[12] We will see God with resurrected eyes; this is the goal of eternity.

The New Heaven and New Earth and the Beatific Vision

Here we must press into the promise of seeing God, the beatific vision. Many times, when we think of heaven,

---

12. Samuel G. Parkison, *Irresistible Beauty: Beholding Triune Glory in the Face of Jesus Christ* (Fearn, Ross-shire, UK: Christian Focus Publications, 2022), 147.

we think of how it has been romanticized by Hollywood. We may imagine clouds and baby angels floating around strumming harps. We may also envision streets of gold and mansions of glory as some old hymns portray. The truth is that Scripture gives us very little detail about our eternal dwelling. However, just how we cannot think about our glorified bodies as the end goal of our resurrection, the point of our eternity is not about us, but rather the triune God. It is not that we will not enjoy our eternal existence, but the highlight of that joy is God Himself.

A temporary mediated glory

The heart cry of Moses in Exodus, should be our heart cry as well, "Great triune God, show us Your glory!" (see Exod. 33:18). This is indeed our hope that we will see Him as He is (1 John 3:2). The problem with our current state, as mentioned above, is that there is no way for us to take in this vision without our glorification. As God tells Moses, no one can see Him and live (Exod. 33:20). Therefore, it takes the transformation of glorification to see the fullness of triune glory. Thankfully, Christ in His incarnation has mediated this glory for us in some sense. Once again, the apostle John is helpful when he testifies, "The Word became flesh and dwelt among us. We observed his glory, the glory as the one and only Son from the Father, full of grace and truth" (John 1:14). Notice the observation of God's glory as through the Word incarnate (Jesus), but it is a glory that comes as the one who is eternally begotten of God (a more helpful rendering of one and only). The apostles testify to the glory of God in the person of the Son, especially as He mediates it to them in His time on earth. The Lord Jesus veils His glory through putting on humanity, and the apostles testify to seeing that glory in the life and acts of the Eternal Son become incarnate.

It is through this same incarnation that Jesus makes possible for believers the full vision of the glory of God. In other words, this is another way in which He mediates God's glory to us through His perfect life, death, and resurrection. As we stated previously, sin's entrance into the world made it so that the unregenerate cannot only not be in the presence of God, but also cannot live in the fullness of His glory. The believer is made ready in the here and now by virtue of being justified by Christ's finished work and are being prepared for the beatific vision in sanctification, while awaiting the fullness of that vision in glorification. The anticipation of that vision is what drives the believer to live a sanctified life now (as we shall see in chapter 6). For now, however, as we focus on the vision, we need to flesh out what the Scriptures tell us concerning it and what that means for the new heaven and new earth dwelling.

The beatific vision proper

We have worked through aspects of the beatific vision in previous chapters and sought to whet the appetite of the believer a bit, but now we must explore this concept more fully. In our contemporary church life, and especially in Protestant circles, we have lost this important doctrine. Concerning this reality, Hans Boersma quips, "the beatific vision no longer fits within the broader framework of our lives."[13] As I stated earlier, heaven, in many ways, is simply set over against hell as the better option. Certainly, it is, but rarely do pastors or theologians contemplate the greatness of the eternal existence with the triune God at the center. It's not that God is not mentioned, but rather that God is a part rather than the whole. As Samuel Parkison says, "There is a place for enjoyment of God's good gifts, even in heaven, but the beauty of the beatific vision is that all of those gifts will be enjoyed in God."[14] I've heard some say that heaven might be boring if all we do is take part in some heavenly church service for eternity—though the angels don't seem to mind (Isa. 6:1–3; Rev. 5:11–12). While it is possible to conceive of our eternal existence as more, it is certainly no less than

---

13. Hans Boersma, *Seeing God: The Beatific Vision in Christian Tradition* (Grand Rapids: Eerdmans, 2018), 17.
14. Parkison, *Irresistible Beauty*, 208.

living eternally seeing God; and if it was only that vision, we would find ourselves completely satisfied in it. The reason is that the hope of the Christian should be (and will be realized someday) the vision of God. As R. B. Jamieson and Tyler R. Wittman express about the Beatific Vision, it is "the eschatological vision of God that . . . renders us blessed . . . at its core blessedness is our highest hope, and it consists in an intimate communion with God that quiets our hearts' deepest longing and fills us with everlasting joy."[15] Jesus Himself gives credence to this hope when He says, "Blessed are the pure in heart, for they will see God" (Matt. 5:8).

Seeing the fullness of God's glory captured the heart and mind of the early church. Going back to one of the earliest fathers mentioned above, Irenaeus, at the very end of his treatise on theology, states that those who are in Christ will "ascend to Him, passing beyond the angels, and be made after the image and likeness of God."[16] It may seem like a familiar statement to us that the believer will ascend to God, but notice that Irenaeus says we will pass "beyond the angels." In one sense, Irenaeus is commenting against those

15. R. B. Jamieson and Tyler R. Wittman, *Biblical Reasoning: Christological and Trinitarian Rules for Exegesis* (Grand Rapids: Baker Academic, 2022), 6.
16. Irenaeus of Lyons, "Irenæus against Heresies," in *The Apostolic Fathers with Justin Martyr and Irenaeus*, ed. Alexander Roberts, James Donaldson, and A. Cleveland Coxe (Buffalo, NY: Christian Literature Company, 1885), 1:567. The Ante-Nicene Fathers.

who would state that those who are resurrected become like the angels and rather that they are finally conformed to the image of God in a way that was not even the status of mankind in the garden. But as such, the ascent to God is also a dwelling with Him because of being conformed in that image that prepares us to be with Him. We gather this truth from what Irenaeus says previously in this section when he writes:

> And in all these things, and by them all, the same God the Father is manifested, who fashioned man, and gave promise of the inheritance of the earth to the fathers, who brought it (the creature) forth [from bondage] at the resurrection of the just, and fulfils the promises for the kingdom of His Son; subsequently bestowing in a paternal manner those things which neither the eye has seen, nor the ear has heard, nor has [thought concerning them] arisen within the heart of man.[17]

Irenaeus is, of course, quoting from 1 Corinthians 6:9 in which Paul is speaking of the mystery of the gospel, but

---

17. Ireneaus, 1:567.

that gospel has as its trajectory and telos the beautiful vision of God in the face of Jesus Christ. It seems wise to include in those writings that God has prepared for those who love Him, the promise of the triune God Himself!

Moving ahead in church history we see Augustine state that the "[beatific] vision is reserved as the reward of our faith; and of it the apostle John also says, 'When He shall appear, we shall be like Him, for we shall see Him as He is.' "By 'the face' of God we are to understand His manifestation, and not a part of the body similar to that which in our bodies we call by that name."[18] The reward of our faith should not be understood as something we earn, but rather the goal of our faith. Augustine employs Paul's words about seeing through a glass dimly now, but we will know then as we are known now (1 Cor. 13:12). As well, he states it is the manifestation of the triune God that the believer sees, and that manifestation in the fullness of God's glory, seen certainly in the glorified incarnate person of Christ, but also in every way throughout the fullness of the new heaven and new earth.[19]

---

18. Augustine, *City of God*, 2:507.
19. Augustine states it thusly, "God will be so known by us, and shall be so much before us, that we shall see Him by the spirit in ourselves, in one another, in Himself, in the new heavens and the new earth, in every created thing which shall then exist; and also by the body we shall see Him in every body which the keen vision of the eye of the spiritual body shall reach." Augustine, *City of God*, 2:509.

The theologian probably most associated with working out the beatific vision is Thomas Aquinas, who said, "The desire of the saints cannot be altogether frustrated. Now the common desire of the saints is to see God in His essence, according to Exodus 33:13, *Show me Thy glory*; Ps. 79:20, *Show Thy face and we shall be saved*; and Jo. 14:8, *Show us the Father and it is enough for us*. Therefore the saints will see God in His essence."[20] It does not serve out purposes here to work through all of the discussion surrounding what it means that "the saints will see God in His essence," but suffice to say, this is the church's historic understanding of the beatific vision. Some may ask, but what about the church today? Michael Allen rightly assesses, "A survey of the vast terrain of modern Protestant divinity evidences a deep abyss: the doctrine of the beatific vision has dropped into oblivion."[21] Including Allen, there are a handful of authors seeking to address the lack of focus upon the vision of God, and I hope to add to the fray here, so that we might see the ultimate end of our existence fulfilled in the vision of God and our enjoyment of eternal communion with Him.

---

20. Thomas Aquinas, *Summa Theologica*, trans. Fathers of the English Dominican Province (London: Burns Oates & Washbourne, 1920-22), "Treatise of the Resurrection": Question 92, Article 1.

21. Michael Allen, *Grounded in Heaven: Recentering Christian Hope and Life on God* (Grand Rapids: Eerdmans, 2018), 59.

Conclusion

The hope of glory is indeed the dwelling of mankind with God, beyond what even Adam and Eve experienced in the garden of Eden, and as furnished by God through the redemptive work of His Son, who not only lived and died on our behalf, but rose again. It is this resurrection hope secured by Jesus Christ's own resurrection that will make us ready for the fullness of enjoyment with God as we see Him face to face. It is with this promise that we turn now to the way in which this reality compels us to live for our triune God today, as we shall see in our next chapter on the sanctifying work that the hope of glory produces.

THE SANCTIFYING WORK OF THE HOPE OF GLORY

"Though we have not Christ now present before our eyes, yet if we hope in him, it cannot be but that this hope will excite and stimulate us to follow purity, for it leads us straight to Christ, whom we know to be a perfect pattern of purity."[1]
—John Calvin

In line with what we saw previously concerning the beatific vision, we must also explore the way in which our hope of glorification influences our lives today. There is a sense in which many believers today are satisfied with

---

1. John Calvin and John Owen, *Commentaries on the Catholic Epistles* (Bellingham, WA: Logos Bible Software, 2010), 207.

the concept of justification in which their eternity is sure but give little thought to the way in which all our salvific hope helps drive our sanctification today. In this way, we see a way in which all our salvation comes full circle. What I mean is that we see here how the hope of glorification motivates our sanctification in the present. We come back to a familiar passage in our book, that hope which Paul gives that all who are justified will be glorified (Rom. 8:29). We recall that in this same passage God is conforming those who are His to the image of His Son. We remember further that the apostle John says, "everyone who has this hope in him purifies himself just as he is pure" (1 John 3:3). When we combine Paul and John's statements, we see the way in which the hope of glorification motivates our sanctification.

Once again, we must emphasize that there is no sense in which our sanctification assures our glorification; that hope is grounded in our justification. Christ has won it all for us. However, the fruit of our justification, the reality of being new creatures in Christ (2 Cor. 5:17), is that we have been given a new desire for the things of God, and as such as Calvin says above, "this hope will excite and stimulate us to follow purity, for it leads us straight to Christ, whom we know to be a perfect pattern of purity." The object of our faith is also the one whose pattern of life we must follow.

Paul tells us to imitate him as he imitates Christ (1 Cor. 11:1). Simply put, with the hope of being fully conformed to Christ in our resurrection, we look to His life as the example for ours. John Gill is helpful when he states:

> This is only owing to the grace of God and blood of Christ; nor that any man can be so pure and holy as Christ is, who is free from all sin, both original and actual; but this must be understood either of a man that has faith and hope in Christ, dealing by these with the blood of Christ for purity and cleansing, with whom and which these graces are conversant for such purposes; or of such a person's imitating of Christ in the holiness of his life and conversation, making him his pattern and example, studying to walk as he walked; to which he is the more excited and stimulated by the hope he has of being a son of God, a dear child of his, and therefore ought to be a follower of him, and walk as Christ walked, in humility, love, patience, and in other acts of holiness; and by the hope he

has of being like unto him, and with him in
the other world to all eternity.[2]

Thus, with this hope for the future we are to live sacrifi-
cially for Him in the present. As Paul writes in application of
what he has laid out in Romans 1-11, in chapter 12 we are to
no longer be conformed to the pattern of this world but be
transformed by the renewing of our minds (Rom. 12:1-2).
We are tempted to find our hope in the things of this world
or in ourselves rather than to have our hope shaped by the
gospel that promises not only that we are forgiven of our
sins, but that we are being transformed into the image of
Christ, which is ultimate in our glorification. Paul goes on
to describe what he outlines as a spiritual act of worship. He
describes it as that which is reasonable service to God. This
makes sense considering God's mercy to save Paul. Love the
Lord your God with everything you are. This is not theoreti-
cal but should be the reality of the life of a true believer in
Christ. Mercy cannot be earned, it is given, but living considering God's mercy motivates us to love and obey Him.
Bearing in mind this idea of lifestyle-worship, Paul goes on
to exemplify what this means. As mentioned above, Paul
says, do not be conformed to this world, do not be shaped

2. John Gill, *An Exposition of the New Testament*, vol. 3, The Baptist
Commentary Series (London: Mathews and Leigh, 1809), 636.

by this age. It is interesting to see what Paul states as the end of Romans 11:36, that glory will be God's to the end of the age. Therefore, we are not to be conformed to this age, but be transformed by the renewing of our minds as we look toward the eternal. We are to remember that God is receiving glory to the end of this age, (and we are in an age that does not want to bring glory to God!), and we are to stand out as those who are conformed to something different.

Union with Christ in Sanctification: Definitive and Progressive

As I said previously, just as one finds the grounding of justification in Christ's righteousness, so too must this be sanctification's grounding. Speaking of the need of both doctrines having their foundation in the believer's union with Christ, Horton skillfully bridges the two concepts of justification and sanctification writing, "To be sure, justification is exclusively extrinsic—the imputation of Christ's alien righteousness—but, more generally, salvation also includes transformation."[3] Horton goes on to speak of this crucial aspect when he says, "such sanctifying transformation rests on Christ and our union with him through faith . . . union

---

3. Michael Horton, *Justification*, New Studies in Dogmatics, vol. 1 (Grand Rapids: Zondervan Academic, 2018), 207.

with Christ [is] the source of sanctification."[4] One should understand that the believer's growth in holiness rests in their justification, but both are grounded in Christ and His finished work. In other words, a believer cannot claim their righteous activities or growth in holiness as their own. There is however a way in which theologians discuss sanctification that needs addressing before proceeding further into the theology of sanctification and union with Christ.

When referencing the "already" aspect of the entirety of salvation, the conversation contains characteristics of justification and sanctification. Often when one hears the term *sanctification* they associate with the idea of growth in holiness. While sanctification certainly implies holiness, we must not overlook the basic meaning of *consecration* and wonder about the definitive aspect of it.[5] David Peterson argues that "sanctification in the New Testament is an integral part of the redemptive work of Jesus Christ [and] is regularly portrayed as a once-for-all, definitive act and has to do with the holy status or position of those who are 'in Christ.'"[6] Considering this observation in light of the pursuit of a

---

4. Horton, *Justification*, 207.
5. *Definitive* is the term used by John Frame. Frame, *Salvation Belongs to the Lord: An Introduction to Systematic Theology* (Phillipsburg, NJ: P&R Publishing, 2006), 214. See also Bruce Demarest, "Positional Sanctification" in *The Cross and Salvation* (Wheaton: Crossway, 2006), 407–8.
6. David G. Peterson, *Possessed by God: A New Testament Theology of Sanctification and Holiness* (Leicester, England: IVP Academic, 2001), 24.

conversation around union with Christ, we see the importance of precision in the matter of understanding sanctification as following justification, but also its definitive nature
as it relates to a completed work. In other words, if one is
united to Christ in His righteousness, this is not only a legal
declaration of the sinner's right standing but also places
them positionally as set apart unto God. As Peterson puts
it, "In the New Testament [sanctification] primarily refers
to God's way of taking possession of us in Christ, setting us
apart to belong to him and to fulfil his purpose for us."[7] This
does not mean that holiness is not part and parcel of this
concept. The idea of an inward change and disposition is
the basis for growth in holiness. If one holds that those who
are in Christ are regenerate and that "the old has passed and
the new has come" (2 Cor. 5:17), this new disposition and
standing is not only true concerning justification, but also
the position of the believer as one who is not only rightly
related to God in righteousness but set apart unto Him in
holiness. This is not to discount the idea of growth in holiness, but rather to consider that justification is the basis for
all the consequential realities for those who are united to
Christ.

---

7. Peterson, *Possessed by God*, 27.

With these matters in mind, there is certainty growth in holiness and the conforming of the believer into the image of Christ. As we have seen, Paul states this definitively in Romans 8:29 when he says, "For those whom he foreknew he also predestined to be conformed to the image of his Son." This leads to needing an understanding of what this conforming to the image of Christ as growth in holiness looks like. The Reformed tradition uses the term *sanctification* oftentimes to speak of this transformation. For instance, the Westminster Confession speaks of sanctification in one sense as definitive when it uses the following phrase, "They who are effectually called and regenerated, [have] a new heart and a new spirit created in them."[8] This language is also tied to the idea of growth in holiness when it goes on to say:

> [They] are farther sanctified really and personally, through the virtue of Christ's death and resurrection, by his word and Spirit dwelling in them; the dominion of the whole body of sin is destroyed, and the several lusts thereof are more and more weakened and mortified, and they more and more

---

8. Westminster Assembly, *The Westminster Confession of Faith: Edinburgh Edition* (Philadelphia: William S. Young, 1851), 73.

quickened and strengthened in all saving
graces, to the practice of true holiness, without which no man shall see the Lord.[9]

The scriptural proofs given in this edition of the WCF
point to a two-tiered understanding of sanctification when
the authors use such a passage as 1 Corinthians 6:9–11,
where Paul outlines a list of vices. Commenting that those
who practice such things will not enter the kingdom of
heaven, Paul reminds the saints of Corinth, "such *were*
some of you. But you were washed, you were sanctified, you
were justified in the name of the Lord Jesus Christ and by
the Spirit of our God" (1 Cor. 6:11 ESV, emphasis added). Of
course, within the context of these definitive statements,
Paul is also concerned with the believers ongoing actions.
He says in 1 Corinthians 6:9–10 that anyone who continues habitually sinning in the areas listed will not inherit
the kingdom of God. Believers, therefore, were to recall
that they had been washed, sanctified, and justified. This
new paradigm of life results in *ongoing* transformation. As I
mentioned earlier, this other side of the sanctification coin
is usually called *progressive sanctification.* While this idea
certainly fits within the realm of sanctification, it seems

---

9. Westminster Assembly, *The Westminster Confession of Faith: Edinburgh
Edition,* 73–74.

better to talk about progressive sanctification in terms of growth in holiness and the promise of being conformed to the image of Christ. This truth speaks directly to the issue of the already/not yet nature of salvation and the need of the believer, through the Spirit, to put to death the deeds of the flesh because we still struggle with sin.

The Believer's Ongoing Battle with Sin

To put it into the form of a question, What does it mean to be united to Christ with all the benefits therewith and still struggle with sin? The WCF helpfully summarizes, "This sanctification is throughout in the whole man, yet imperfect in this life; there abideth still some remnants of corruption in every part; whence ariseth a continual and irreconcilable war; the flesh lusting against the Spirit, and the Spirit against the flesh."[10] The scriptural proof given in the version of the WCF quoted is Galatians 5:17, in which Paul says, "For the flesh desires what is against the Spirit, and the Spirit desires what is against the flesh; these are opposed to each other, so that you don't do what you want."

One could easily see the comparison as well with Romans 7:14-23, where Paul seems to spell out this inner

---

10. Westminster Assembly, *The Westminster Confession of Faith: Edinburgh Edition*, 74.

struggle in more detail. F. F. Bruce comments on Galatians 5:17 that "The conflict between the two [Spirit and flesh] in human experience belongs to that 'eschatological' tension which, so long as believers remain in mortal body, is inseparable from their life in Christ."[11] This tension is what Paul seems to indicate in the latter part of the Romans 7 passage mentioned above. In his frustration over not doing what he desires and doing what he does not desire, he bursts forth exclaiming, "What a wretched man I am! Who will rescue me from this body of death? Thanks be to God through Jesus Christ our Lord!" (vv. 24–25). It seems as if Paul is reminding himself that one day, he will be free from the body of death (glorification), but then he resolves that for now "with my mind I myself am serving the law of God, but with my flesh, the law of sin" (v. 25). The hope of which Paul speaks in Romans 7:25 is in line with the hope of glorification, when we no longer battle with sin. Thomas Schreiner helpfully comments:

> Since believers have not yet experienced the consummation of their redemption, they are keenly aware of their inherent inability to keep God's law. When believers contemplate

---

11. F. F. Bruce, *The Epistle to the Galatians: A Commentary on the Greek Text*, New International Greek Testament Commentary (Grand Rapids: Eerdmans, 1982), 244.

their own capacities, it is clear that they do not have the resources to do what God demands. In encountering God's demands, we are still conscious of our wretchedness and inherent inability. The struggle with sin continues for believers because we live in the tension between the already and the not yet. . . . All believers are frustrated by their failure to keep God's law and long for the day when redemption will be completed and perfection will be theirs.[12]

The idea of the believer's ongoing struggle with sin leads to the question of what his life should look like in the already/not yet tension. Bavinck states simply, "The life of Christ is the shape, the model toward which our spiritual life must grow."[13] This definition is helpful concerning the shape of the Christian life and puts forth the idea then of transformation. We may recall again where Paul states that "we all . . . beholding the glory of the Lord, are being transformed into the same image from one degree of glory to another" (2 Cor. 3:18 ESV). The idea of "being transformed

---

12. Thomas R. Schreiner, *Romans* (Grand Rapids: Baker Academic, 1998), 390–91.
13. Herman Bavinck et al., *Reformed Ethics: Created, Fallen, and Converted Humanity*, ed. John Bolt (Grand Rapids: Baker Academic, 2019), 315.

into the same image" begs the question of "which image?" The context seems to point to the idea of the glory of the Lord. Murray Harris submits, "when Christians are transformed, the change is essentially inward . . . and becomes visible only in their Christ-like behavior."[14] Therefore, the believers union with Christ is a crucial component of their justification, their being set apart unto God (definitive sanctification) and their growth in holiness (progressive sanctification). If it is true that the believer is united to Christ in their growth in holiness, and this is as Harris says to do with their Christlikeness, it is further, as Bavinck contends, a matter of imitating Christ.[15] He goes on to point out the passage that likely comes to mind, "Be imitators of God" (Eph. 5:1). There is then also Paul's admonition in 1 Corinthians 11:1, "Imitate me, as I also imitate Christ." Put another way one could say, "Mimic me, but only in the ways I mimic Christ."

An interesting parallel is possible when one considers that Christ's perfect obedience, wins for us the same capacity. Though still in a fallen nature, believers are awaiting the day when they can perfectly imitate Him in His humanity. Nevertheless, believers are still awaiting that final delivery, not only from the power of sin (from which they have

---

14. Murray J. Harris, *The Second Epistle to the Corinthians: A Commentary on the Greek Text*, New International Greek Testament Commentary (Grand Rapids: Eerdmans, 2005), 316.
15. Bavinck, *Reformed Ethics*, 315.

already been delivered), but also its presence. This raises the question not only of what is realistically "attainable" for the believer, but also what capacity the believer plays in their growth in holiness. It is perhaps wise to answer the second question first. The short answer to the question of participation is, yes. But this "yes" needs nuance. R. Lucas Stamps provides the following understanding, "'progressive sanctification' involves the process of moral transformation in the life of the believer by the inner working of the Holy Spirit in cooperation with the believer's own efforts."[16] The crucial portion of this understanding that needs addressing is the idea of the "believer's own efforts." The Reformed tradition makes great pains at stressing that even this effort is rooted in God's grace alone and therefore by faith. Any effort put forth on the part of the believer is only because God has worked first and enabled him to do so. Walter Marshall proclaims:

> Holiness in this life is absolutely necessary
> to salvation, not only as a means to the end,
> but by a nobler kind of necessity, as part of
> the end itself. Though we are not saved by
> good works as procuring causes of it, we are

---

16. R. Lucas Stamps, "Faith Works," in Matthew Barrett et al., *The Doctrine on Which the Church Stands or Falls: Justification in Biblical, Theological, Historical, and Pastoral Perspective* (Wheaton, IL: Crossway, 2019), 508.

saved to good works, as fruits and effects of
saving grace, "which God has prepared that
we should walk in them" (Eph. 2:10).[17]

Marshall highlights the relationship between the effec-
tiveness of grace in the life of believer and the way that works
out in his life. John Owen famously comments, "The choic-
est believers, who are assuredly freed from the condemn-
ing power of sin, ought yet to make it their business all their
days to mortify the indwelling power of sin."[18] Immediately
following, as if he knew the temptation would be for the
Christian to lean on human works, he states, "The principal
efficient cause of this duty is the Spirit."[19] Of course, Owen is
basing this off Romans 8:13, "if by the Spirit you put to death
the deeds of the body, you will live," and Colossians 3:5,
"Put to death what belongs to your earthly nature." Owen
captures the already/not yet stating, "Indwelling sin always
abides whilst we are in this world; therefore, it is always to
be mortified."[20] What then is the action of this mortification?

---

17. Walter Marshall, *Gospel Mystery of Sanctification* (New York: R. Carter
& Brothers, 1859; Modernized, formatted, annotated, and corrected by
William H. Gross www.onthewing.org, 2019), Kindle locations 1854–1857.
18. John Owen, *The Mortification of Sin* (1656; repr., Carlisle, PA: Banner of
Truth, 2022), 6.
19. Owen, *The Mortification of Sin*, 7.
20. Owen, *The Mortification of Sin,* 10.

Though Owen has written much, a brief summation of his work is necessary.

First, one cannot accomplish any putting to death of sin without the Holy Spirit. Owen states that the "renewing of the Holy [Spirit] . . . is one great way of mortification; he causes [the believer] to grow, thrive, flourish, and abound in those graces which are contrary, opposite, and destructive to all fruits of the flesh, and to quiet the thriving of indwelling sin itself."[21] He goes on to show that this does not diminish the obedience of the believer, but shows that the means of this obedience is through a regenerate heart, which by the power of the Spirit, "He works upon our understanding, wills, consciences, and affections . . . so that his assistance is an encouragement to the facilitating of the work, and no occasion of neglect as to the work itself."[22] Therefore, the work of killing sin cannot be attributed to mankind. It is the Holy Spirit who continues to shape the regenerated person toward mortification. Owen also addresses the matter of killing sin concerning extent in the present life showing that, "to mortify a sin is not utterly to kill, root it out, and destroy it, that is should have no more hold at all nor residence in [the believer's] heart. It is true this that which is

---

21. Owen, *The Mortification of Sin,* 20.
22. Owen, *The Mortification of Sin,* 20.

aimed at; but this is not in this life to be accomplished."[23] Owen is agreeing with the tension of the already/not yet aspect of growing in holiness. Thus, the believer is responsible for submitting to the Spirit's work by God's grace and enablement in this life, but that the tension of battle rages on until glory.

This concept fits within the already/not yet paradigm which we have come to time and again in this book. We are already being conformed to the image of Christ, just as one day we will be fully conformed to that same image. Here, we outline what is stated in 1 John 3:2-3 when John elates that those who have the hope of being like Christ when we see Him as He is, also purify themselves in view of that reality. John's encouragement concerning Christ's appearing is couched in the middle of his letter-wide theme of those who know God not pursuing sin. John uses phrases like "walking in light" instead of "darkness" to indicate proper fellowship with God and being cleansed from sin because of the blood of Jesus (1 John 1:7). Within the same context, he calls believers to confess their sins because we all sin and Christ has provided forgiveness of sin (1 John 1:8-2:2). John then goes on to say that this fellowship with God is expressed as well in the way we love the brothers and sisters of the church

---

23. Owen, *The Mortification of Sin*, 24-25.

and that those who love God and brethren do not love the world (1 John 2). He then begins speaking on the appearance of Christ and the believer who has "confidence and [is] not ashamed before him" (2:28), because they are made righteous because of His righteousness. This can be seen as grounding our glorification in our justification. Once again, we see where Paul relays this truth in Romans 8:29-30:

> For those he foreknew he also predestined to be conformed to the image of his Son, so that he would be the firstborn among many brothers and sisters. And those he predestined, he also called; and those he called, he also justified; and those he justified, he also glorified.

Notice Paul's take on the doctrine of glorification. He speaks of the conforming of believers to the image of Christ, which seems to be that which is happening presently, yet those whom God justified will also be glorified—the completion of the conforming of believers to the image of Christ is glorification. Just before this is Paul's call to the believer to live according to the Spirit and not according to the flesh (Rom. 8:1-14) but then explains that those who are in Christ will suffer, like Christ suffered and that we (along with creation) groan for the redemption of our bodies. This redemption is what we rightly call *glorification* in theology. Therefore, we see the correlation of our justification, sanctification, and glorification. That we who have such a hope would live as Christ lived, suffering with hope, and purifying ourselves as we look to that hope. It is not with anticipation of earning anything, since Christ has already earned it for us, but rather with anticipation of our final transformation in being conformed to the resurrected image of the eternal Son. The Reformed confessions (e.g., Westminster, Second London Confession) speak of this hope in various ways; sometimes as the hope of the resurrection and sometimes in the language of judgment. The Second London Confession relays the hope of resurrection as "the last day, such of the saints as are found alive, shall not sleep, but be changed and all the dead shall be raised up with the selfsame bodies, and none other; although with different qualities, which shall be united again to their souls forever."[24] Subsequent to the statement about the resurrection, concerning the coming judgment the same confession states, "for then shall the righteous go into everlasting life, and receive that fullness of joy and glory with everlasting rewards, in the presence of the Lord," and

---

24. 2LCF, 31.2.

As Christ would have us to be certainly per-
suaded that there shall be a day of judgment, both to deter all men from sin, and for
the greater consolation of the godly in their
adversity, so will he have the day unknown to
men, that they may shake off all carnal secu-
rity, and be always watchful, because they
know not at what hour the Lord will come.[25]

We see from these summaries of our faith the hope and
joy of glorification, as well as the motivation of purity that
comes from that hope. Therefore, the believer who has been
justified, and is being sanctified, will be glorified the very
moment we behold the beauty of God in the face of Jesus.
And the response to this in the here and now is that we
would put on Christ Jesus as our garment of righteousness,
purifying ourselves as He is pure as we await the beatific
vision. This means that even as we live with our eyes upon
this world proclaiming the truth of the gospel, the gospel
hope of our salvation also points our eyes heavenward,
with the hope and comfort of His appearing and with such
anticipation calms our fears, but also compels us by such
great grace and hope living our lives for Him awaiting His

---

25. 2LCF, 32.2, 3.

return![26] We should now look at the ways God has provided for us to be sanctified as we await our glorification.

God's Ordinary Means of Sanctifying Grace

John Calvin said there are certain marks of a true church.[27] Some have referred to these marks as the ordinary means of grace. Perhaps some who hear the term "means of grace" are shocked because they assume that it means grace imparted as a means of justification. This concept comes from a Roman Catholic view, rather than what the early church and the Reformers meant by it. Rather than the elements themselves containing grace, rather God's grace works through the sacraments.[28] Calvin identifies the means

---

26. Some of this material in this chapter is taken from an article I wrote for Union Theology's blog, "The Hope of Glorification," Jason B. Alligood, June 27, 2022, https://www.unionpublishing.org/resource/the-hope-of-glorification/.

27. Calvin says, "Wherever we see the Word of God purely preached and heard, and the sacraments administered according to Christ's institution, there, it is not to be doubted, a church of God exists [cf. Eph. 2:20]." John Calvin, *Institutes of the Christian Religion & 2*, ed. John T. McNeill, trans. Ford Lewis Battles, vol. 1. The Library of Christian Classics (Louisville, KY: Westminster John Knox Press, 1960), 1023.

28. Louis Berkhof says it this way, "While the grace of God generally operates mediately, it is not inherent in the means as a divine deposit but accompanies the use of these. This must be maintained in opposition to the Roman Catholics, the High Church Anglicans, and the Lutherans, who proceed on the assumption that the means of grace always operate in virtue of an inherent power, though their operation may be made ineffective

of grace as preaching the Word, and the administration of the sacraments, namely: baptism and the Lord's Table. It is imperative that we investigate these as means that not only spur on sanctification in our lives, but also as those means that point to Christ's return and our glorification.

Preaching the Word

Paul tells Timothy in 2 Timothy 4:2 to "preach the word; be ready in season and out of season; correct, rebuke, and encourage with great patience and teaching." We can already see the way in which this God-ordained event is meant to encourage the believer into sanctified living by the grace of God. This means correction, rebuke, and encouragement by the Word of God (coupled with His Spirit) will sanctify the believer. However, lest we miss the connection with our theme of glorification, we should note that Paul's "solemn charge" to Timothy is considering "God and Christ Jesus, who is going to judge the living and the dead, and because of his appearing and his kingdom" (2 Tim. 4:1). Paul has the end in mind; the very appearing, judgment, and kingdom of God is the motivation for Paul to call Timothy to the preaching of God's Word as fundamental to his calling. Calvin

---

by the condition or attitude of the recipient." Berkhof, *Systematic Theology* (Grand Rapids: Eerdmans, 1938), 608.

says, "for although he now reigns in heaven and earth, yet hitherto his reign is not clearly manifested, but, on the contrary, is obscurely hidden under the cross, and is violently assailed by enemies. His kingdom will therefore be established at that time when, having vanquished his enemies, and either removed or reduced to nothing every opposing power, he shall display his majesty."[29]

Beyond these realities, Paul also explains to Timothy that "the time will come when people will not tolerate sound doctrine, but according to their own desires, will multiply teachers for themselves because they have an itch to hear what they want to hear. They will turn away from hearing the truth and will turn aside to myths" (2 Tim. 4:3-4). These words remind us that God not only saves us but keeps us and that He does so by means. The means that God uses here is the preaching of the Word and He keeps us by His Word from wrecking our faith. Therefore, we can say that God's Word is a means of sanctification for us as we see those around us succumbing to myths, we focus upon God and His truth as we await the coming of His kingdom at which point, we will be glorified and fully conformed to the image of Christ.

---

29. John Calvin and William Pringle, *Commentaries on the Epistles to Timothy, Titus, and Philemon* (Bellingham, WA: Logos Bible Software, 2010), 252-53.

However, we must acknowledge that preaching the Word is what pastors usually do; it is ordinary. As Michael Horton points out, God does not use extraordinary means to accomplish what He desires in us, but ordinary means.[30] This does not mean that those means do not carry extraordinary significance in the life of the Christian. It is by these means, and here specifically, the preaching of the Word that the believer is rebuked, corrected, and encouraged in their faith. It is to this end that Paul presses onward, even in these encouragements to Timothy. Just moments later in his letter Paul speaks of his own departure into God's presence where he speaks of "the crown of righteousness, which the Lord, the righteous Judge, will give me on that day, and not only to me, but to all those who have loved his appearing" (2 Tim. 4:8). Notice the last phrase "to all those who have loved his appearing." Something awaits the saints in the future that they love in the present. That something is the hope of the Lord's appearing to which the preaching of God's Word points. The anticipation of the appearing of the Lord and the glorifying of the saints is the end to which Christians in Paul's day longed for and contemplated consistently. As we continue to relay throughout this book, salvation is not just about justification as an end, but rather the beginning of the

---

30. See Michael Horton, *Ordinary: Sustainable Faith in a Radical, Restless World* (Grand Rapids: Zondervan), 2014.

whole salvation enterprise. God has justified us, is sanctifying us, and will glorify us. The Word preached is a means of God's sanctifying grace in that we are reminded of the grounds of our justification in Christ, we are rebuked, corrected, and encouraged in our faith until we stand before the treasure of the triune God Himself, who we shall see at His appearing.

The contrast in these verses are clear, there are those who will love this present world and pile up for themselves teachers who will scratch their itching ears and turn aside to myths (2 Tim. 4:3-4) Then there are those who, like Paul himself, love the appearing of Christ and as John Gill quips, "his appearing at his second coming; which is to be loved, and so looked for by the saints, not only because it will be glorious in itself, in its attendants and consequences, but will be of great advantage to the saints; Christ will appear unto salvation to them, and so to their joy; they will appear with him in glory, and be like him, and enjoy the everlasting vision of him."[31] The preaching of God's Word ought to have an already/not yet sanctifying work in the life of the Christian. As we traverse toward the beatific vision, our hearts are set aright on this path as often as the Word of God is preached by God's servants and appropriated by us

---

31. John Gill, *An Exposition of the New Testament*, vol. 3, The Baptist Commentary Series (London: Mathews and Leigh, 1809), 341.

according to God's Holy Spirit. We do this so that our lives reflect the change wrought in our heart by Him to prepare and excite us for that day! There is no lesser degree of truth concerning baptism and the Lord's Supper, which we look at next.

The Ordinances of Baptism and the Lord's Supper

Baptism, along with communion, have no short history of debate, not the least of which is whether we should call them sacraments or ordinances. For the sake of our reading, we shall forgo the debates and make some general assumptions about the nature of both.

Baptism

Baptism is clearly taught in Scripture, especially as a means of entry into the community of the saints. Jesus brings this to light in His commission to the disciples when He states, "Go, therefore, and make disciples of all nations, *baptizing* them in the name of the Father and of the Son and of the Holy Spirit, teaching them to observe everything I have commanded you" (Matt. 28:19–20, emphasis added). No doubt these words are familiar to the majority of the readers of this book. Baptism is nestled in the middle of the formation of God's New Testament church. The New Testament shows earlier examples of baptism, such as John the Baptist's baptism of repentance to which Jesus Himself submits so that all righteousness may be fulfilled (Matt. 3:15). However, at the beginning of the New Testament church we see that baptism becomes the outward expression of the inward reality of salvation and is the initiatory step into the church.

"Making disciples" is the thrust of Jesus's command, but the how is in the three modifiers to the command: to go, to baptize, and to teach. This becomes the mode of the Great Commission as is seen in the rest of the New Testament. "Going" is the practice that is exemplified in the ministry of Paul. He goes to different regions and doesn't just evangelize. He remains in places, starting churches, and teaching them about the Lord. In 1 Corinthians we see that even though he had not baptized many, he had baptized some. This was clearly part of the practice he had in the early days of planting churches. As we will see in a moment, this is no different than the beginning of the New Testament church in Acts. But there is no question as to what the apostles were going to do as they went on their way making disciples and then passing that on to others as the commission which Jesus gave. And it was not just make converts—it was make disciples, with the correlating practice of baptism.

Peter indicates that there is a correlation between baptism and the conscience of the person who has believed in the resurrection of Jesus Christ, when he writes, "Baptism, which corresponds to this, now saves you (not as the removal of dirt from the body, but the pledge of a good conscience toward God) through the resurrection of Jesus Christ" (1 Pet. 3:21). He does not mean salvation regarding justification, but instead a means of sanctification. As Karen Jobes says, "[Peter] reminds his readers that at baptism they pledged to live in relationship with God, which would result in a good conscience before him."[32]

Thomas Schreiner states, "Peter repudiates an *ex opere operato* [meaning that baptism—or any other sacramental action—saves by virtue of the action itself being performed] view of baptism, for he immediately qualifies the statement that baptism saves. It does not save mechanically or externally as there are magical properties in the water. Peter comments that the mere removal of dirt from the body does not bring salvation, demonstrating that the water itself does not save. Baptism is only saving if there is an appeal to God for a good conscience through the resurrection of Jesus Christ. In other words, baptism only saves because it is anchored to the death and resurrection of Jesus Christ.

---

32. Karen H. Jobes, *1 Peter*, Baker Exegetical Commentary on the New Testament (Grand Rapids: Baker Academic, 2005), 255–56.

The waters themselves do not cleanse as is the case when a bath removes dirt from the body."[33]

Paul includes baptism in his letter to the Romans thusly:

> What should we say then? Should we continue in sin so that grace may multiply? Absolutely not! How can we who died to sin still live in it? Or are you unaware that all of us who were baptized into Christ Jesus were baptized into his death? Therefore we were buried with him by baptism into death, in order that, just as Christ was raised from the dead by the glory of the Father, so we too may walk in newness of life. For if we have been united with him in the likeness of his death, we will certainly also be in the likeness of his resurrection. (Rom. 6:1–5)

It refers in the one sense to the internal and to the external which represents the internal. Schreiner again is helpful, "The reference to baptism is introduced as a designation for those who are believers in Christ. Since unbaptized Christians were virtually nonexistent, to refer to those

---

33. Thomas R. Schreiner and Shawn D. Wright, eds., *Believer's Baptism*, New American Commentary Studies in Bible and Theology (Nashville: B&H Publishing, 2006), 70.

who were baptized is another way of describing those who are Christians, those who have put their faith in Christ. Thus, Paul is saying here that *all Christians* have participated in the death and burial of Christ, for all Christians had received baptism. To posit that the baptism mentioned here is simply metaphorical . . . or baptism in the Spirit . . . rather than water baptism is incorrect. . . . Roman Christians would have inevitably thought of water baptism since it was the universal initiation rite for believers in Christ."[34] There was no such thing as an unbaptized first century believer. We have so separated what is the absolute necessity for someone to be born again, (i.e., what is the bare minimum someone must do to be saved). And by that, we have stripped the command of Jesus in Matthew 28 down to the steps one must take to receive Christ, rather than seeing that Christ commands us to repent and live our life for Him as is demonstrated initially through the waters of baptism.

And it is in this way that we understand baptism as a means of grace. We are not saying that Baptism confers saving grace, but rather as Steve Wellum writes:

> in the practice of baptism there is the bless-
> ing of God. In our obedience to Christ and

---

34. Thomas R. Schreiner, *Romans* (Grand Rapids: Baker Academic, 1998), 307–8.

our public act of confessing Him, the Lord of the church pours His love and joy into our hearts. When baptism is practiced, as a sign of the believer's union with Christ, the Holy Spirit strengthens our faith and encourages us to press on. In our celebration of this [ordinance] in the presence of the body of Christ [the church], the people of God are encouraged in their commitment to the Lord and to each other.[35]

Further as we press into this means, we see the eschatological hope—the hope of glorification—in the resurrection symbol of one coming up from the waters as one who has been buried in Christ's death and yet raised like Him. Perhaps this understanding goes unnoticed in our day, but it is significant as we consider the already/not yet paradigm: those who have been buried with Christ will also be resurrected as He has. Certainly, there is a spiritual significance with that idea—we have been spiritually regenerated/raised with Christ—but there is also the significance of the future resurrection wrapped up in it as well.

---

35. Stephen J. Wellum, "The Means of Grace: Baptism," in *The Compromised Church*, ed. J. H. Armstrong (Wheaton: Crossway, 1998), https://www.the-highway.com/articleJan99.html.

The Lord's Table, Communion

Our hearts often forget what God has done for us. As we come to the Lord's Table, we are reminded not only of what Christ did, but also of His return. The Lord commands us to do this until He comes again. The sweet communion of the saints with the Lord at His table reminds us that there will be a day when we will dine with Him at the Marriage Supper of the Lamb.

Additionally, the Lord's Table is a time of sanctifying grace in that it calls us to reflect upon Christ's death and the reason He had to go to the cross. Paul, imploring the Corinthian church to understand and practice the Lord's Supper properly states the following:

> whoever eats the bread or drinks the cup of the Lord in an unworthy manner will be guilty of sin against the body and blood of the Lord. Let a person examine himself; in this way let him eat the bread and drink from the cup. For whoever eats and drinks without recognizing the body, eats and drinks judgment on himself. (1 Cor. 11:27–29)

So Christians are to examine themselves to see that they do not despise the Lord's death and confess their sin as they consider those truths. However, this is not the end of the matter at the Lord's Table. Earlier in his instructions Paul says, "For as often as you eat this bread and drink the cup, you proclaim the Lord's death until he comes" (1 Cor. 11:26). We are once again reminded of the gospel-centrality of the table in "proclaiming the Lord's death," but notice that last phrase, "until he comes"! Though there may be differences about the theological meaning of the Lord's Supper, most Christians agree that we are to have our eyes turned upward in that event, looking toward that glorious day.[36] I love what John Gill says about the hope of the future with God found in the Supper:

> this assures of the certainty of Christ's second coming; as it leads back to his coming in the flesh, suffering and dying in our stead, and thereby obtaining redemption for us; it leads forward to expect and believe he will come again, to put us into the full possession of the salvation he is the author of; when there will be no more occasion for this

---

36. Here is not the place to examine all the various views of the Lord's Table. See Thomas R. Schreiner and Matthew R. Crawford, *The Lord's Supper: Remembering and Proclaiming Christ Until He Comes* (Nashville: B&H Academic, 2010).

ordinance, nor any other, but all will cease, and God will be all in all.[37]

This reality is emphasized even more as we realize that the Lord gave us tactile reminders of His physical body, which was not only hung on a tree for our sake, but also that He has been glorified in His humanity and we will one day experience His presence in that sense. Putting it bluntly, we will be able to touch Christ! We shall behold Him; we shall be with Him! This should instill hope in the life of every believer. As we partake of the ordinary means of grace, we look to our sanctification now in the true hope of our glorification that is to come.

Church Discipline

Looking back to Calvin's marks of a true church, he does not include church discipline. It is implied, however, when one considers the nature of the church and her ordinances. The bottom line is that church discipline determines the status of one's hope from the perspective of the church. When Jesus tells Peter that he has been given the keys of the kingdom and when that is then coupled with church discipline,

---

37. John Gill, *An Exposition of the New Testament*, vol. 2, The Baptist Commentary Series (London: Mathews and Leigh, 1809), 691.

one of the ways in which God hems us in to the reality of our glorification is the accountability we have within the local church.

The purity of one's life and the purity of the church is dependent upon the exercise of church discipline. It is the Lord Jesus Himself who outlines this practice for us in Matthew 18:15–20. When any of us sin against our brother or sister or is seen by a brother or sister, we are to confront that person about their sin or be prepared to be confronted about our own. If they repent, the relationship is restored. If, however, they do not, we are to take along two or three witnesses to establish the truth concerning that sin. If the sin is established as truthful and the person still refuses to repent, then the church is told, and they are to lovingly call that person back to repentance. But if they still refuse to listen to the church, then they are to be treated as a Gentile and a tax collector, as if they are unregenerate. The way in which Jesus also speaks of this is that if that decision is made by the church, that heaven agrees with that decision (Matt. 18:18). This level of accountability in the church is always difficult and always sad, but the reality is in that moment, we are calling the unrepentant sinner to believe the gospel. We are pointing them back to the law of God and the grace of God as the only means for them to be reconciled to God.

The point of this section on the means of grace is to display the way in which God brings about sanctification in our life, a pursuit of purity in light of Christ's purity as we await His return, when we will be made complete in His likeness. Instead of looking for extraordinary means by which God is conforming us to the image of Christ, we are looking to the means that He has already given.

Conclusion

We return once again to the summary statement of our chapter, which is what John explains as the action of those who have the hope of seeing Jesus and being like Him: "everyone who has this hope in him purifies himself just as he is pure" (1 John 3:3). Just as we look to Christ's return with a longing to be like Him, so we should long to be like Him today, which is pure. One aspect of the hope of our glorification is how it motivates us today to be like Jesus. We do not do this so that we might earn something from God; we cannot do that! Instead, we pursue purity out of a sense of gratitude for what God has done as He guides us by His Word. Some of those who have come before us speak of a trifold way of thinking about what God does for us through the law and the gospel: guilt, grace, gratitude.[38] For the person who is unregenerate, the law brings guilt; it exposes us to the holiness of God against which we measure ourselves and find ourselves lacking. Not only this, but it condemns us; it brings the guilt associated with our sin against a Holy God. It is then by God's grace that we are set free from slavery to sin and by which we are given the righteousness of Christ and declared right standing before God. Then, as those who are made new by God's grace, we live in gratitude of what He has done for us, enabled by Christ's righteousness and by His Spirit to live according to the law, not as a means to earn anything from God, but again, from a place of gratitude.

As we consider the law post-conversion as that which guides the Christian and that which the Christian does from the place of gratitude, we can summarize it the way Jesus does when He says we are to love the Lord our God with all of our heart, soul, mind, and strength and to love our neighbor

---

38. These three—guilt, grace, gratitude—are attributed as a summary of the Heidelberg Catechism, but explicitly stated in question and answer 2, which states, "What must you know to live and die in the joy of this comfort? Three things: first, how great my sin and misery are; second, how I am set free from all my sins and misery; third, how I am to thank God for such deliverance." The comfort of which this question speaks in summary is that those who are in Christ belong to Christ and are cared for and preserved in the faith by Him as found in question and answer 1 of the Heidelberg Catechism.

as ourself (Matt. 22:37–40). In other words, the way we purify ourselves is to live like Jesus lived. Jesus, in His humanity, lived in every way pleasing to the Father and for the sake of loving others, which in both cases drove Him to the cross (John 3:16; 4:34; 10:14–18; 14:31; 15:13; Rom. 5:8).

THE HOPE OF THE FUTURE THAT BRINGS HOPE TODAY

"The glorified shall never have fear, nor cause of fear of any loss: they shall ever be with the Lord."[1]
—Thomas Boston

A s we reach the final chapter, we now present the apex of our study, the hope of hope. This phrase may seem redundant, but it highlights the reality of what we are pressing into in this book. The hope of glorification brings hope today! What we look forward to in our glorification brings hope for our present life.

---

1. Thomas Boston, *The Whole Works of the Late Reverend and Learned Mr. Thomas Boston* (Aberdeen, Scotland: George and Robert King, 1848), 8:339–40.

I remember as a child when I would have a nightmare, I would run to my parents' door and wake them. Usually, my mom would be the one to comfort me. These were her words: "think about heaven and all that awaits us there." She had a sense that all would not be well this side of glory and that my only true comfort and rest would come through what awaited me in heaven. Of course, in my young mind I would conjure up the images that were most fascinating to me: streets of gold, giant gates made of pearl, mansions in which I would dwell with my family and being reunited with my loved ones who were already there waiting for me. As I have grown older, I realize that these are secondary to the real delight of heaven, dwelling with the triune God.

As Thomas Boston writes in more detail from our quote above, "They shall attain the full persuasion, that nothing shall be able to separate them from the love of God, nor from the full enjoyment of him forever."[2] As we have said previously, the triune God is the focus of our eternity and as with other aspects of our redemption; He is the center of our hope here and now. As with resurrection hope—which is a piece of our glorification—if it were not so we are above all men most to be pitied (1 Cor. 15:19). What is the hope of glorification if not final vindication of our triune God's name?

---

2. Boston, *The Whole Works of the Late Reverend and Learned Mr. Thomas Boston,* 8:340.

All that we have considered thus far is fruitless if we do not find comfort in these truths in our daily walk. If this were a sermon, perhaps we can see this chapter as the application of all we have studied together.

In this chapter we will recall some of the broader categories of our study to cultivate the hope of glorification as we close out this book together.

Not Wishful Thinking

We need to be reminded that the hope of which we speak is not a wish, but a confident certainty. Our confidence is not in anything that we have done, but in what the triune God has done in saving us, not just in the sense of being declared right standing with a Holy God through the perfect life, death, and resurrection of the Son, not just in the way that God is currently conforming us to the image of the Son, but also in the reality of coming into the fullness of our salvation at glorification. As the author of Hebrews states, "faith is the reality of what is hoped for, the proof of what is not seen" (Heb. 11:1). If we state that we believe something, it is not a hope that is dormant, but a hope that is alive. As Calvin says, "What would become of us were we not supported by hope, and did not our minds emerge out of the midst of darkness above the world through the light of God's word and of his Spirit? Faith, then, is rightly said to be the subsistence or substance of things which are as yet the objects of hope and the evidence of things not seen."[3] Since we are certain of this hope by faith in the God who has already justified us, is sanctifying us, and will glorify us, we live as those who truly believe such.

Hope Rooted in Justification

I would be remiss if I did not remind us that this hope of glorification is rooted in our justification. The finished work of Christ is the ground upon which our glorification is secured. As we face the absolute wrecked nature of this world in sinfulness, the beginning of any hope is the perfect life, death, and resurrection of the Lord Jesus Christ. As those who are born in Adam and therefore born in sin, we are faced every day with our own sinfulness and the sinfulness of others, not to mention the effects that sin has had on creation. The breaking in of the newness of life is because of the gospel. Paul says in Romans 6:4, "Therefore we were buried with him by baptism into death, in order that, just as Christ was raised from the dead by the glory of the Father, so we too may walk in newness of life." Here we see that we

---

3. John Calvin and John Owen, *Commentary on the Epistle of Paul the Apostle to the Hebrews* (Bellingham, WA: Logos Bible Software, 2010), 262.

have a first resurrection in anticipation of a second resurrection. Just as we were raised to new life spiritually, we one day will be raised to new life physically. For those of us who have trusted in Christ, we are united to Him; we therefore speak of our union with Him. This is Paul's overture again and again when he uses the phrase "in Christ."

Free from Sin

In the first chapter, we observed how a part of our glorification is that sin will be no more. Regarding our glorified dwelling, the apostle John writes, "Nothing unclean will ever enter it, nor anyone who does what is detestable or false, but only those written in the Lamb's book of life" (Rev. 21:27). This is at least a part of the hope of glorification. So, when we sin today, we know that "if we confess our sins, he is faithful and righteous to forgive us our sins and cleanse us from all unrighteousness" (1 John 1:9). And as we consider the truth that sin will be no more, this hope should motivate us in glorifying God in this way now. In one sense, as we all deal with "sin that so easily ensnares us," those things which weigh us down now, that we seek to "lay aside" (Heb. 12:1), our sense of hope is encouraged because there is coming a day when we will no longer have that fight. As above, when Paul speaks of this struggle, his freedom from the flesh—the hope of his resurrected body—is in Christ alone. We, of course, do not diminish this hope of sinlessness by seeking to earn anything from God, but rather we remember what Christ has already accomplished and live in gratitude considering that finished work. Take heart, Christian, there is coming a day when you will no longer deal with sin. The way that hope motivates us now is, though we long to see the face of God in Christ Jesus, we live before Him now!

Finally, and Fully Conformed to His Image

In the second chapter, one of the details we emphasize is being conformed to the image of the Son who is the image of God (Rom. 8:28; 2 Cor. 4:4). As a part of the beatific vision, we hope in the participation of the divine life of God as it is true in the resurrected Son. A key verse in our study is 1 John 3:2, "We know that when he appears, we will be like him because we will see him as he is." This hope is difficult to get our heads wrapped around because we have not experienced it yet. However, whatever way in which we sense that we are not fully in communion with the triune God right now, our hope is in the day when there will be no sense of separation from God, but full communion with Him.

Therefore, as we look forward to this certain hope, we partake in the ordinary means of grace that constantly point us to that perfect union. We should take the opportunity of participating now in the means that God has provided, such as witnessing the baptism that reminds us of Christ's life, death, and resurrection, which is symbolic of the saints' own resurrection hope. When we partake of the Lord's Table, we are communing with Him with our eyes turned toward heaven in the hope of dining with Him when He promises to drink the cup again with us. As we are exhorted and corrected through the preaching of the Word as the preacher reminds us of this hope, we cast our eyes upward to the Word made flesh coming to receive us to Himself. As we fellowship with the saints in His mediated presence now, we look to the fellowship we will have together with all the saints with Him one day.

Seeing God Face to Face

Once again, even as we consider the promises above, we look to the hope of the beatific vision, the cry of Moses to see God's glory (Exod. 33:18), the desire of David to see His beauty (Ps. 27:4), the vision of Isaiah seeing the Lord seated on His throne as the angels proclaim (Isa. 6:1-3), the longing of the disciples as they look for Jesus in the sky

(Acts 1:9–11), the certainty of Paul that the incorruptible will inherit heaven (1 Cor. 15), the visitation of God as written by Peter (1 Pet. 2:12), the dwelling of God with mankind that the apostle John witnesses in his vision (Rev. 21). We will be participants in this real event. The hope of seeing God is the ultimate realization of the longing of the saints. Even if we hope in other aspects of eternity, our focus is upon the One who is Creator of all things. I hear many Christians longing to be with their departed loved ones, which in and of itself is not wrong. However, our hope is to be with them in the eternal state of worship in the presence of the triune God without fear of death (Exod. 33:20).

One element of this truth that is hard for us to grasp is that the vision of God is beyond what anyone other than perhaps Jesus Himself experienced in humanity.[4] Dwelling with God and the blessed vision of God seems to be more than what Adam and Eve experienced in the garden, the theophanies of the Old Testament, even more than the incarnation, since John writes that we have yet to see God as He is (1 John 3:2–3). As Allen summarizes that through the progress of Scripture, "there is a strong and growing sense

---

4. There is much discussion over whether Jesus experienced the beatific vision in His incarnated life. If you're interested in a comparison of two views, see William Chami, "Did Jesus Possess the Beatific Vision During His Incarnation?: A Comparative Essay on the Perspectives of Thomas Joseph White and Thomas G. Weinandy," *Aristos* 4, no. 1 (2018), Article 5.

in our blessed hope is a beatific vision, namely that God will be fully and finally visible to his people."[5] Further, we press into the truth that the hope of this experience is what motivates us today to live purely as He is pure.

As we consider what it means to be pure as He is pure, it is important that we keep this hope of seeing God ever before us. If this is the ultimate hope of our glorification, we should contemplate it now. You may have heard it said, "that person is so heavenly minded, they're no earthly good." While I understand the sentiment, I believe what I have shown in this book is that in order to be any earthly good (loving God and loving neighbor as we should) we must be heavenly minded. The apostle Paul helps us when considering the affliction we face as those who believe the gospel. He states, "Therefore we do not give up. Even though our outer person is being destroyed, our inner person is being renewed day by day. For our momentary light affliction is producing for us an absolutely incomparable eternal weight of glory. So we do not focus on what is seen, but on what is unseen. For what is seen is temporary, but what is unseen is eternal" (2 Cor. 4:16–18).

We notice that Paul calls the afflictions he and the Christians of his day were facing as "momentary" and

---

5. Michael Allen, *Grounded in Heaven: Recentering Christian Hope and Life on God* (Grand Rapids: Eerdmans, 2018), 75.

"light." When we consider the kinds of persecution and affliction that Christians, not to mention Paul, went through in those days, we would call them anything but "light." The idea is not that these are not real trials for them, but rather that those trials are insignificant in comparison to the eternal *weight* of glory. I love the wordplay Paul uses here; light afflictions compared to the weightiness of glory. The word for *weight* can be translated as *fullness*. Therefore, the hope of our glorification promotes a way of living for today.

The Sanctifying Work of Our Hope

As we consider how the hope of glorification outweighs our current trials, this theme pushes us further into God's work of sanctification in our lives as we await that glorified reality. As we have seen, those who have such a hope, purify themselves as He is pure (1 John 3:3). Our glorification is not dependent upon this purity, but God's finished work in Christ guarantees our progress in being conformed to Jesus and thus continues to prepare us for our glorification. We gratefully obey the Lord out of our love for Him because He has changed us, and we follow what He has given us as a way of life for our good now with a view of our ultimate joy in Him in the future.

The way in which God sanctifies us is by the ordinary means He has given us—namely the preaching of God's Word and the ordinances: baptism and the Lord's Table. Each of these have an eschatological piece to them. As Paul says, we "work out your own salvation with fear and trembling. For it is God who is working in you both to will and to work according to his good purpose" (Phil. 2:12–13). In other words, we are, by God's gracious means submitting ourselves to Him, by His Spirit with our eyes fixed on our future hope. These already realities point us to the future not-yet of our hope.

Our Hope for What Will Be Shapes Our Today

Finally, I want to remind you that whatever you're experiencing today is not the end. God, in His infinite grace and mercy, has not only redeemed you for Himself in this life and is not only conforming you to the image of His Son currently, but is working all of these things out for your good and His glory, which culminates in your glorification which has the end goal of you seeing the glory of God in the face of Jesus Christ (Rom. 8:28–30; Matt. 5:8; 1 John 3:2). This not only ought to be something we believe that is "out there" in the future. We should contemplate the reality of it as the truth of what motivates our hope today.

Brothers and sisters, look heavenward, you will one day see the glory of God in the face of Jesus Christ. We know that we are currently the children of God, and though we do not fully grasp what we will be like, we do know that when we see Him, we will be like Him (see 1 John 3:2)! Beyond this event we will always be with the Lord, dwelling with Him, without sin, in His presence and seeing His beauty, united to Him in glorification through Christ. Christian, hope in your glorification!

ABOUT THE AUTHOR

Jason B. Alligood (PhD Midwestern Baptist Theological Seminary) is an assistant professor of theology at Cedarville University. Previous to his time as a full-time professor, Jason was a pastor in various capacities for twenty-seven years, the last of which was as the teaching pastor of Fellowship Bible Church in Peoria, Illinois. Jason has been married to Amber since 1997 and they have three grown children who are all happily married and two grandchildren.